TRUE
COMPASS

 FriesenPress

Suite 300 - 990 Fort St
Victoria, BC, V8V 3K2
Canada

www.friesenpress.com

Copyright © 2021 by Sandra M. Lowe
First Edition — 2021

Author photo credit: Kevanna Studios

ISBN
978-1-5255-9653-7 (Hardcover)
978-1-5255-9652-0 (Paperback)
978-1-5255-9654-4 (eBook)

1. BODY, MIND & SPIRIT, MINDFULNESS & MEDITATION

Distributed to the trade by The Ingram Book Company

THE LED BY GRACE SERIES

Led by Grace
The Ley of the Land
True Compass

IN PRAISE

". . . After two back surgeries and chronic pain, life is hard sometimes. Most of the time I felt that I was stumbling around in the dark. After reading Sandra's book, *Led by Grace*, a small crack opened and let in light and understanding. Sandra's next book, *The Ley of the Land*, made that opening wider . . . It has given me hope."

—Kerry-Lee Labbe, Soul on a Journey

"Sandra Lowe's books are an invitation to anyone . . . to embark on their own journey to discover the larger Self in everyday life . . . [Sandra] is not afraid to share her vulnerabilities, her doubts and her confusions . . ."

—Richard Meech, Documentary Filmmaker

"Living with chronic pain, I keep going back to *Led by Grace* again and again. It has been a life-saving resource. When I read one of Sandra's meditations, I become deep in the meditation myself—and I am pain free."

—Shelley Duplessis-Skouris, Medical Attendant

". . . By crossing the innumerable bridges of life and trusting (letting go), Sandra Lowe has travelled metaphorically and spiritually to places I can only imagine."

—Rodney Sim, Investment Executive (Ret)

"... I was reading Sandra's book at 3 a.m. one night and began to feel calm and reassured that I was going to be able to cope [at an unsettling time] ... The effects of her writing are still with me."

—Louise Moran, Registered Practical Nurse

"*Led by Grace* ... speaks of divine love, self-acceptance and trust in universal consciousness, and if the reader allows, opens up a dialogue with one's own soul."

—Ann Fenlon, Pharmacist, MSc. Energy Medicine

"So often we conceal our true selves. What a gift to have Sandra express her inner thoughts and feelings, allowing us to feel heard in our own lives."

—Lorraine Nelemans, Reflexologist

"... Sandra gave us beautiful descriptions of her experiences in her meditations. Her ability to share these experiences opened doors for us to be on our own spiritual path ..."

—Patty, Meditator

"... Sandra Lowe's sharing of her meditations reminded me in a most beautiful way that grace is a profound force that is ever present, inspiring anyone who is brave enough and vulnerable enough to be open to it ..."

—Mary Lou Gignac, Regulatory Body Executive (Ret)

"A journey of self-discovery, a true marvel of bravery."

—Anna Marie Bougie, Reiki Master

TRUE COMPASS

*A Journey
to Inner Peace*

SANDRA M. LOWE

For all those seeking inner peace

Your inner knowing is your only true compass.

—Joy Page

TABLE OF CONTENTS

AUTHOR'S NOTE

I use the term Spirit as interchangeable with Universe, God, Creator, Source. I refer to Spirit within all of us as our Soul. I also capitalize words (such as Light, Grace, Essence) that I use as synonyms for Spirit and Soul.

LETTER TO THE READER

Dear Reader,

It wasn't my idea to be here. Getting here was overcoming my fear of being here. The genesis of this book dates back to the spring of 2001, when a Reiki Master suggested I might like to explore that technique of energy healing. From that moment, my life began its journey to inner peace.

What was my life like before the "moment"? It was, by outward measures, a charmed life. I had four wonderful children, a like-minded husband, good health, a network of family and friends, financial security and had enjoyed a successful career in the investment industry. But not all was rosy. In early 1993, I had two nocturnal grand mal seizures, both unexplained. I was embarrassed and thought my life, as I knew it, had ended. (The truth is that other than taking medication, my life has been unaffected and seizure-free.) And then in 1995, I suffered a depression; once again, I was embarrassed. Fortunately for me, with help, the depression didn't last too long, but I remember the feeling. In addition, about the time of the "moment," my husband and I were beginning our separation.

Amicable though it was, letting go of our history together, especially with children, was difficult. My inner life was beginning to unravel, catch up with itself: happiness was not lasting, guilt was drowning me, I didn't know what I wanted or needed. I couldn't find my heart or my voice.

What was the "moment"? During that first Reiki treatment, I saw a series of colours of the rainbow. Perhaps that doesn't sound remarkable, but the experience set me on a journey beyond my imagination. With each subsequent Reiki session, my meditations grew in complexity. I met guides who took me on journeys, teaching me lessons along the way. I became an avid reader of spiritual books, and my meditations would often reflect aspects of their lessons. I learned to meditate on my own, giving me the opportunity to receive more guidance whenever I wanted. I soon began to experience events in my life that paralleled my meditations, confirming that I was being guided by something beyond me. My journey became an examination of my entire life. No rock was left unturned; no wound, no matter how old, was left to fester.

True Compass is a selection of my chronological meditations from June 2002–October 2004. At the time of each meditation, I wrote down every detail, never thinking you would ever read them. But I unconsciously knew it was important to do so both for you and me; writing this book has been part of my journey. I follow each meditation with a discussion focusing on the key message(s) I have gained from each. I hope my interpretations allow you to experience and absorb the lessons more fully, while also leaving you space to find other messages in the meditations that speak to you.

During the meditations in *True Compass*, Spirit guided me to share my story, and now, 16 years later, here I am. My story is not about how to meditate but about the teachings I was given in my meditations, what I did with the lessons and how they guided me to inner peace. This book is intended for you to receive these lessons, see how they may apply to your own life and perhaps become a model for you to change whatever is keeping you from inner peace. Our personal stories are not the same, but our desire for inner peace bonds us together.

I wish the best for you,
Sandi

PART ONE

Quiet the mind, and the soul will speak.
—Ma Jaya Sati Bhagavati

1
MODEL HOME

We shall not cease from exploration
And the end of all our exploring
Will be to arrive where we started
And know the place for the first time.
—*T. S. Elliot*

June 26, 2002

I am wearing a white flowing dress sitting on a cobblestone beach with a large cliff to the left. It's very quiet; the ocean is calm, and the sun is warming me. After a while, I see a boat being rowed to shore by ten oarsmen. A galleon is in the distance. The boat comes ashore near me, and one of the men waves for me to come on board. No one is talking.

I step into the old boat. It looks like in the movies where the oarsmen are chained together and must row through starvation and fatigue. But, while the men are all sweaty from working hard, they are pleasant looking. They row me out to the galleon.

A rope ladder is dropped over the side. I'm scared as I climb up because the rope ladder is wobbly. I freeze halfway up but then continue and am helped over the side. The captain silently greets me. Several men lead me to my room on the top deck.

The ship is old and wooden, but my room is new and fresh with pale yellow walls, a mantel and the bed in an alcove. I notice a window with a view of the ocean. It is so still that I can hardly tell where the blues of the water and sky meet. I see what I think are pictures on the other three walls but then realize that they are windows with the same open view. I can see out in all directions. It is a beautiful, calm room.

The men bring me my luggage, a large trunk. Inside are carefully wrapped framed pictures of my children. I place them on the mantel and begin to cry. I am so upset because I've left my children and am sailing away.

We sail for many days with no conversation, but the men take good care of me.

Finally, we sight land.

The captain talks for the first time, "You should go ashore."

The crew line up and individually say goodbye. We have an emotional farewell.

"Thank you for helping me," I say as I hug the men who have taken good care of me.

"No, you have taught us so much." I don't know what I've done, but I'm touched by their comment.

When they row me to shore, I realize we've landed on exactly the same beach I left earlier. I had never left the children; they would always be there, and I would always be there. An incredible sense of peace comes over me.

Soon, the children join me on the beach. We swim for hours with the dolphins, hanging on to their fins. Afterwards, we have a picnic feast and watch the sunset.

The children ask, "Where do we go now?"

I don't really know but say, "This way," and lead them down the beach and through a very open forest. At the other end is a grassy meadow with a house in the distance. We walk to it and see it's a shack. The children play outside it while I walk away and meet the monk guide of my first meditations. I tell him all that has happened, and when I turn back to look at the shack, it has become a beautiful small house with wonderfully maintained gardens. The children are laughing and playing with each other.

The children and I walk down to a small river, crossing it by jumping from rock to rock and walking on fallen branches. When someone needs help, I am there. We make our way to the mouth and paddle away.

Discussion

I am connected with my Soul on the tranquil beach. The galleon represents my life. I am collected to return to my life to understand how to live with inner peace.

My quarters on the top deck are a model for living Heaven on Earth. The room symbolizes my Soul and the alcove, my humanity. While in human form, there is not one without the other, and they are equally key to living with inner peace.

The room of my Soul is fresh, calm and clutter-free with a panoramic view to the seamless connection between the sky and the water, symbolically where Heaven and Earth meet. The alcove, with only a bed, is similarly calm with only my healthy thoughts and beliefs. My Soul is guiding my life.

When I live in my quarters, I trust that I will be safely taken to where I am to go and am given everything I need for my journey. My life flows as it is intended both for my best interests and the best interests of others. Whenever this flow is blocked by my unhealthy thoughts and beliefs, I need to return to the model of my quarters.

This meditation takes place a week before our separation, and having the children only half of the time weighs heavily on me. Spirit addresses my distress and teaches me that the children will always be with me, whether physically or not. This is incredibly helpful for me at the time.

I arrive back where I started and know my life for the first time. The children and I swim with the dolphins, and a shack, the second image of how I see my life, transforms into a house of beauty and abundance. I see blessings in all aspects of my life and know that anything is possible.

2

DESCENDING THE MOUNTAIN

One's destination is never a place,
but rather a new way of looking at things.
—Henry Miller

August 28, 2002

I am on a mountain peak looking over a magnificent valley to snow-covered mountains. The sky is bright blue, and birds are flying overhead.

I stand up and stretch my arms to the sun and bring warmth through my body. I bury my feet in the ground to get the warmth from Mother Earth.

An old man comes climbing up the rocks. He is wearing a burlap robe, has a balding head and a long flowing white beard.

"What is your name?" I ask.

"Joshua."

"Are you from the Bible?"

"No, just from the village below."

"I thought the village was Tibetan," I say because he doesn't look Tibetan.

"It is, but I live there too," he says.

I invite him to sit beside me and ask, "What is it about this place that makes it so spectacular? Is it the serenity, the mere magnificence of the scenery?"

He says, "For me, it is my connection to it. Sometimes I feel connected to the rocks; the fluids in my body are calm, and I am grounded. Sometimes I am connected to the birds; I feel lighter, and my body fluids are in motion."

"How did I get here? I didn't climb the mountain."

"You have climbed your own mountains to get here. Some people never come up."

He notices that my feet need to be massaged, so he warms them with a tender massage.

"I can tell from your feet that you always lead with your right foot. You need to start to lead with your left foot," he says.

We decide to head down to the village. Joshua says, "I take a different path down each time, and each one presents a trial."

He leads the way, but it's incredibly steep and dangerous with sheer drops and overgrown pathways. He gets ahead of me, leaving me alone. I'm afraid and terrified of falling as I look down into the blackness below. I carefully lower myself down on a rope, hands sweating and heart racing. I remember Joshua telling me that I have to lead with my left foot; eventually, I feel a shelf with my left foot and ease myself onto it.

But the ledge is very narrow along a sheer wall with few handholds. My back is to the cliff, and I edge myself along, leading with my left foot. I come upon a short section where there is no ledge. I want to be facing the wall to stretch across, but then I'd be leading with my right foot. This concerns me, but I know I have to go on. I turn around and reach my right foot over. I freeze, sprawled across the cliff. I have no leverage to push off with my left foot and no handholds to pull myself forward. Below me is blackness. I start to cry and am terrified. I realize I have to relax, so I will myself to calm down. When I am calm, I know I have to just move. I make it across and carefully shuffle to an opening where Joshua is waiting; I am so thankful and relieved to see him.

As we continue along, he has me lead with my left foot. We arrive at a store, and I see images in my mind of an eagle feather, a lamp and a horse. I find them in the store and buy them.

I hear, "Guided by the power of light."

I lead my horse as we walk on. After a while, I am weary, so we find a place to rest under a tree.

Joshua asks, "Are you inwardly or physically weary? You can be weary just in body, but if you are inwardly weary, you will be physically weary too."

"I am inwardly weary."

"You can ride your horse when you become weary."

After resting, we carry on and find ourselves in a brightly coloured room. I line up behind people waiting for their ceremony of rebirth. When it's my turn, I try to ask questions about what is happening, but the man seems a little short with me. I realize he has a long line of people. He directs me to a woman who is very kind and helpful, but I leave the room without having a ceremony.

Joshua and I sit on a bench before entering the modest village where he lives. We then walk among the people, and I see that everyone is doing their part for all to have a modest life. Joshua is the only non-Tibetan, but everyone accepts his presence.

Discussion

I am connected with my Soul on the mountaintop; the village below represents my daily life. I need to descend the mountain to bring this awareness of my Soul into my life.

The beginning of the descent is very frightening, and I quickly lose Joshua—this section of the journey is one I need to travel alone. But Joshua has given me all I need to safely make it through the most difficult of challenges. I am to lead with my left foot. The right brain (intuition) controls the left side of the body. When I symbolically lead with my left foot, my Inner Knowing is my guide.

Once reunited with Joshua, the way becomes easier, as I have travelled through my fears. Next, I am guided to buy an eagle feather, horse and lamp. The eagle feather represents Spirit, guiding me and reminding me of my Soul. The horse represents my inner power and strength to overcome any roadblocks along the way. The lamp lights my way so I can safely travel the path I am to take. I now have all I need for any future journey.

I have been shown the process to live with inner peace. However, I do not understand the final step, the acceptance of conscious awareness of my Soul in my life. I will need to take different paths down the mountain, which take a multitude of forms, in future meditations. I will safely make my way through different challenges and begin to bring my meditations into my life—have a new way of looking at things and live with inner peace.

3

STEPPING OUT

Just like a snake, we must shed
our past over and over again.
—Buddha

October 2, 2002

I am sitting in a field with pipers playing on
various hills around me. The music is beckon-
ing me to dance. I hold up a crystal to the sun,
and as it glistens and reflects the rays, I climb
the hill and dance around. Then it becomes
dark and I lie down. The pipers come closer
and circle me as they play.

Joshua comes up the hill.

"Are we on the same hill?" I ask.

"No. I have walked for some time. Stand
up," he says.

"I can't. My whole body feels too heavy, and
I can't move."

"You need to get out of your skin."

He demonstrates by taking off his skin. I feel under my chin for the start of the zipper, but I can't find it. He comes over and uses his fingernail to scratch the zipper free. I unzip my skin, from my chin down my chest and stomach, down my left leg, up my back, over my head and down my face back to my chin. Fully unzipped, I step out of my skin. It lies in a pile and looks like snake skin.

"Do I look different?" I ask.

"You have a glow."

"I don't notice a difference in you."

"Either you can't see it, or my skin had not needed to come off. The skin that you shed harboured all that was harmful in you."

"What happens to my shed skin?"

"It will decay into nature like all living things. What was in your skin?"

I think for a while. "Guilt," I say.

We sit down around my pile of skin, and he asks, "Is guilt in this skin?" About one-third of the pile rises up and dissipates into the air.

"What else is in there?" he asks.

I think again and say, "Shame."

"Is shame in this skin?" he asks. Again, about one-third of the pile rises up and disappears.

I suggest competitiveness and dishonesty, but only a tiny puff rises up for each. After that, I have no more ideas.

Joshua calls for reinforcements, and two others come to sit with us. We all hold hands around my shed skin. It's some time before "rejection" comes to me.

"Is rejection here?" Joshua asks. The remaining skin rises up and disappears.

I feel wonderful now; my new skin feels both physically and spiritually light.

"Am I now free of them?" I ask.

"Probably not. This may be only the first layer."

I stand up, open my arms to the sun and feel the warmth coming into my body, all the good things that it needs. I feel I need water, so we find a lake where I swim and delight in being in the cool, shiny water. When I get out, I hold my arms out and watch the water evaporate off.

"Think of something nice," he says. I do and feel wonderful.

"Now think of something unpleasant." I feel constricted and tense; my chest is tight.

"Keep unpleasant experiences on the outside. Use your skin to protect you. These things will affect you but don't bring them inside and harbour them."

I have difficulty getting rid of the negative feeling that I brought to mind, but when I do, a lightness comes over me.

I start to feel pain and pressure in my head. I adjust my head, and when I do, the pain and pressure disappear.

"Don't be afraid to change your position. Things change. Be flexible and don't get stuck," Joshua says.

I leave Joshua and am wandering through a beautiful open forest. I feel incredible, able to overcome any negativity with such peace.

Someone I am uneasy with walks toward me. We pass without words, and I still feel wonderful. Nothing entered me, and when I look back, I can see that healing is taking place in them as well.

Discussion

The challenge to shedding my skin lies in freeing the zipper at my chin, my voice. My negative internal dialogue has buried my zipper so deep that my guide must free it. I need to find new inner dialogue—the dialogue of my Soul.

I will need to shed layers of my skin over and over again as it continues to collect my unhealthy thoughts and beliefs. Discovering what lies within each layer allows me to see the threads that intertwine and repeat themselves. I can see my ongoing roadblocks as well as my progress.

4

HIDING IN THE ALCOVE

How can I begin anything new
with all of yesterday in me?
—Leonard Cohen

October 9, 2002

I am sitting cross-legged, gazing across at snow-covered mountains. I notice something shiny on a mountain peak, like the sun reflecting off a mirror. I feel the warmth and power of this beam of light move through me. It's incredible how wonderful I feel with this energy—except for a horizontal line of pain just below my rib cage. The pain isn't severe, more like a heaviness, half-moon shaped and extending from the left to the right side of my body and from the centre to the front of my body. I concentrate on bringing the beam to this area, but I can't relieve the heaviness.

A man and woman hover above me. I join them and look down at myself. I still can't seem to get rid of this line of heaviness, and I can't move on until I have. I need to go back into my body.

I enter my mouth and find my torso filled with water. I swim down and see a block of wood. I wiggle and shove it, but the block won't budge. I swim up, gulp air and go back down with a saw. I cut away the large central part, swim up and throw it out my mouth.

My stomach area feels so much lighter, but I still have the outer section attached to my skin. I go back down with a chisel, free one end of the block and pull it away from my body. I feel instant relief, but as I keep pulling it away, the first section starts to hurt again. I realize that I haven't sewn up the gaping wound. After the wound is stitched, the pain goes away. I continue to pull the block away, sewing up the wound as I go. When I'm finished, I swim up with the rope-like remains of the block and throw it out my mouth. But then little tentacles of pain start to radiate from the incision.

The man and woman say, "These are parts of the block trying to grow again. You must continue to cut them out. But now it's time to move on."

They take me to a totally white room. "This will be your new shelter; design your windows, doors, walls, floors, ceiling as you want."

I say, "I want earth floors to maintain contact with Mother Earth and an alcove to shelter myself from anyone negative who comes in. I want lots of windows and an open section in part of the roof. I want the front door to open to a downward sloping pathway so I can see people approach and decide whether to let them in. There will be a side door that leads from the past."

They ask, "Who should live here?"

At first, I assume the children but then realize that only I am to live in it; others would be visitors.

"How do I get things done?" I ask.

"You leave your to-do list outside the door and only bring in what you can do. Never more, never less. You will get everything done that you need to."

Someone I have some difficulty with comes to my front door. I let them in, and I feel good. They are glowing and then evaporate into a tunnel of energy.

Discussion

I unknowingly create my house using Spirit's model of my quarters on the galleon (see "Model Home"). But I change the design with a side door leading from the past, giving my ego access to all of my unhealthy thoughts and beliefs. My ego thinks it is large enough to fill my room and tells me it will protect me in the alcove. But not only does shielding myself in the alcove imprison me, I bring all the negativity in with me; my calm alcove on my galleon becomes cluttered.

I need to remove this side door of yesterday by cutting it out block by block and sewing the wounds with the thread of forgiveness. Here, I have taken out a block related to someone I have some difficulty with. They now enter the front door, not the side door of the past, and I see their Light.

My Soul is constant, unwavering—my room never changes. But my alcove does, depending upon the balance of my healthy and unhealthy thoughts and beliefs. I need not have an alcove with only healthy thoughts to experience inner peace in my life—that would be enlightenment—but the condition of my alcove determines the degree. Remembering my Soul guides me to clear out my alcove.

5

THE RIGHT DIRECTION

If we do not change our direction, we are
likely to end up where we are headed.
—Chinese Proverb

December 4, 2002

"For several weeks, I haven't been able to meditate because my mind has been far too cluttered, and I can't seem to let go."

A guide says, "You need to let go of the past, the outside world of what's going on today, and blank your mind."

I'm not feeling sad but feel a tear forming. Yet it never rolls down my face.

I ask, "Do I need to go inside my brain to see what is going on?"

"Ask yourself."

I ask and receive, "Yes."

My guide leads the way to my brain and opens a door with a key. He hands me the key.

"You now know where the door is so go in any time."

Inside my brain, there is a low hum of activity. Some people are busy at various stations, but others are doing nothing or reading papers because that part of my brain is idle. I see moving white lights like the northern lights.

I interpret this inactivity as telling me I need to exercise my brain more, which is exactly what I have been thinking lately. I say to my guide, "I have to get out of my brain because I feel like I'm directing."

I am immediately out of my brain, and my mind wanders and questions.

I feel a strong, painful pull of my head to the right. I then hear my guide's flute on my left and feel my head pull that way as I follow the music to where my guide is waiting. The pain is completely relieved.

"You have been heading in the wrong direction, a dangerous direction for you. Follow me on the left path."

Discussion

During meditation, my necessary functions, such as breathing, are continuing, but my endless number of thoughts are on pause. My ego begins to question, so I leave the stillness of my meditative mind; I have followed my ego to the right, a dangerous direction that results in pain.

I follow the music to the left, where my guide awaits me. Now I am free from pain.

6

SAFE WATERS

In all of nature no storm lasts forever.
—Wayne Dyer

December 12, 2002

I meet my monk guide at a crossroads.

He says, "We have been along each of these paths going in the four directions. We have to travel on a new type of path."

We sit down cross-legged, facing each other.

"Close your eyes, clear your mind and travel whatever path presents itself," he says.

I find myself in a storm with black thunderous clouds. I'm lying prone on the wooden decking of a lifeboat with a sail, clinging to the railing. Waves are crashing over the boat, rocking it back and forth. I'm frightened and do not, or cannot, get up to sail the boat.

My guide says, "Look around and see if you can see anything."

In the distance on the horizon, I see a bright sky and the edge of the storm. The wind is pushing the boat toward the calmer water. But I don't get up; I'm afraid to let go of the handholds. Eventually, the boat drifts to calm, sunny waters. I can see the storm's fury behind me.

I am back sitting cross-legged with my monk. I want to go on another journey, but I can't feel or see anything. I stay like this for some time, and even with my guide putting his hands on either side of my head to help me, still nothing comes up.

Another guide comes along and sees that I need help. He puts his body around the two of us.

"Perhaps you don't need a journey, just total quietness," he says.

He puts his hands on my knees to quiet my lower body, and I fall into a very deep meditation.

"You have to meditate each day to calm yourself and rid yourself of negative energy that will only fester and become toxic; it clogs your pores, not allowing freshness to get in and negative harmful energy to get out."

I am so peaceful.

Discussion

When I was in my quarters on the galleon, floating in the calm water, my life was flowing as it is intended. Here, my ego has thrown me overboard in a raging storm. But, importantly, I am in a lifeboat I can pilot.

I am guided to see that my storm does end, and I am drifting to calm waters. And yet, I am still afraid to let go of the handrails, let go of what my ego tells me is true. If I do not deal with the reason for my storm, I will go right back into the same one, perhaps with different people and situations, but the same storm.

If I had been able to let loose my fear and sail the lifeboat, I would have reached calm waters much faster. By meditating daily, I connect with my Soul and receive guidance on ridding myself of my ego toxins. Without the weight of my ego, I am able to stand up and sail myself to calm waters.

Throughout my life, I will experience personal storms. All of my storms will end, but their severity and duration will depend upon me letting go of whatever had created each one. As I learn to address my ego issues, my storms will become increasingly less frightening and shorter.

7

LIGHTEN UP

As soon as you trust yourself, you will know how to live.
—Johann Wolfgang von Goethe

December 30, 2002

"My reactions to others' behaviours have covered me with a blackness over the past couple of weeks."

I hear, "Let go of what is upsetting you."

Waves of negativity surge through my body, down my arms and out my fingers. I am so calm.

"Seal your fingers from negativity and let in only the Light. Feel the energy, your empowerment."

I feel the Light surge through my body. I can see Light in my toes and in my fingers.

"Believe."

"But I do believe already."

"Believe in yourself. Trust yourself, trust your feelings and do not judge yourself.

"You are safe. You do not have to be afraid. Your Soul is always safe, but It is so buried by your fear that you do not know It is there."

An older man in a brown cloak appears and tells me to walk on the clouds. I leave my heavy body and, feeling very light, walk through the clouds. I come upon a large party where people are gathered in small groups. Everyone is laughing and having a wonderful time. I join a group discussing all of the beauty they see around them—the birds, the trees, the lakes. I tell them about seeing woodpeckers on my hike yesterday as well as about hugging a tree and feeling that I was inside it.

I leave the party and continue walking on the clouds. The older man says, "Essences of people are in the clouds."

"Why don't I see anyone or bump into them and hurt them?"

"Look around. An Essence will not harm."

I see bits of Light flittering around like fire-flies, but no one is hurting anyone or interfering with them.

From time to time, I lose my lightness and go back to my body. It feels so heavy, with a tightness in my sternum/throat area.

The older man tells me to feel light again. At first, it takes a while; my legs do not want to leave my body. I finally convince them that I can't walk without them. I'm running joyfully through a grassy meadow laden with daisies.

The older man meets me. "You need to lighten up a bit, don't take everything so seriously—laugh and enjoy life."

We play on the swings and get an ice cream cone. We ride on a Ferris wheel, but while the sights from above are magnificent, I don't like the feeling of coming down. Instantly, we're off it.

My monk guide then comes, and we talk about my not being with him recently.

I say, "I haven't been on any bridges lately."

"That is only because you haven't stepped onto them." He takes me to a precipice. "Are there bridges here?"

I know that bridges are only visible when you step onto them.

"If I were alone, I wouldn't think so. But because you are with me, I think there probably are."

"There are always bridges; you just have to believe and look."

I look around and don't see bridges but an entire platform surrounding the precipice.

"When you are in a difficult place, feeling anxious, move to a safe platform and shield yourself," he says.

I move from the precipice to the platform and feel the empowerment of my Light through my body. I look down at my toes and see my Light twinkling through my toenails. I pray that I can feel this lightness, joy of living and peace at all times.

Discussion

I have been swept into a vortex of self-pity and judgement both of myself and others; I am figuratively living in my now-cluttered alcove. I believe in my Self, my Soul, in my meditations, but the fear of losing myself, of living in this blackness, is blocking me from believing and trusting in myself in my life. I need to bridge the gap between the two by bringing my meditations into my life.

To move toward this, I have to lighten up by changing what I am fixating on and see the beauty, the fun and joy around me. I will start to feel more balanced, better able to remember lessons I have been taught. I need to walk on invisible bridges that take me to my learning. And I need to step onto platforms that will keep me safe.

Believing and trusting in myself does not mean believing that I am right and others wrong. It means trusting my Inner Knowing. I am then able to see why others are behaving as they have, why I am behaving as I have and what fears and hurts we are both expressing. The gap between my meditations and my life is bridged so that I believe and trust in myself.

8

THE DANCE
OF OUR LIVES

We are not human beings having a spiritual experience.
We are spiritual beings having a human experience.
—Pierre Teilhard de Chardin

January 15, 2003

My right leg begins to feel a little different, and I realize it wants to leave my body. I let it go, and my leg floats up and starts dancing above me to the music. It keeps calling for the rest of my body to join in. My left leg leaves, and my two legs are performing Riverdance.

"Music is a key form of communication," I hear.

Various instruments call for different parts of my body. My hands leave to play the guitar. Next, my arms leave to join my hands, then my torso to connect with my legs and arms.

They say, "Come on up, head. It's great here and we need you." My head floats up and joins them, leaving my physical body behind.

I am dancing away out-of-body when I notice brilliant iridescent yellow and red shapes and designs that are in constant motion making a most magnificent scene.

"Where am I?"

I hear, "You are in a different reality. To the Beings here, this is their reality."

I realize that the Beings are the more solid yellow and red columns. I move among the colours feeling relaxed, happy and thankful. I then see iridescent green/blue and move through it. I come to iridescent white, like mother of pearl. I put my hand into it and see the green/blue mix with the white until I am totally immersed in it, and I too become white. I twirl around with my arms in the air trying to bring everything into me.

I become distracted either by something I need to do or by some pain in my chest, and I'm immediately back in my physical body. I tell myself to replace the negative thoughts with positive thoughts. I'm able to get back to the iridescent colours but keep slipping back to my body.

A bald eagle comes and hovers beside me. I hold out my arm, and he ever so gently takes my wrist in his talon and flies away with me.

We fly in peace, with his huge wings flapping slowly and powerfully, making a whooshing sound with every beat.

He stops flying, cocks his head to look me in the eye, then nuzzles his beak into his chest and gives me an eagle feather. I look at his yellow talons and see yellow flowing out in lines from each talon. The lines get wider and wider until the whole sky is a brilliant yellow. He lets me go, and I float in this sea of yellow.

I am then going up tight circular stairs in some kind of monument and become quite tired but know that I have to go on. Eventually, I get to the top of a lighthouse. I step outside onto the two-metre platform and see an array of iridescent colours, almost more brilliant than before.

A splat of red/yellow iridescence lands on my right shoulder like someone has thrown paint at me. I smear it all over me, and as I do, I lose the appearance of my body. I float, dance, twirl and envelop myself in the ever-brighter colours. I move along and come to green/blue and then to purple/pink. Finally, I arrive at white. I wonder if the movement of the colours is affected by how quickly I move. I move slowly and then quickly, but my iridescent colours undulate, roll, shape-shift in a constant manner. In this reality, speed of movement does not matter; everything is in a calm and constant state.

As I'm twirling around and touching what I believe are other Beings, I suddenly feel resistance in my movement, something denser. I then know that I am not alone; I have met a new friend and am among friends.

My new friend and I take form and dance the dance of our lives. All around us are white iridescent columns.

I thank everyone in my new world.

Discussion

Spirit calls me to leave my body. The first time, I am twirling around among the formless Beings. The second, I go a step further, becoming formless and finding the colours more brilliant than before.

Spirit then calls me back to my body. I feel the density of my familiar physical world and know that I am not alone. My new friend and I dance the dance of our lives— the awareness that we are Beings having a human experience. I find happiness, joy, freedom, lightness, peace, calmness and true connection with others. And I see the Light in others.

Spirit has given me the precious gift of experiencing this ultimate awareness. All of my lessons lead me toward this ideal. I am blessed with each forward step I take, recognizing that my journey will be ongoing throughout my life.

9

THE REFLECTION

Having everything is just an expression
of complete inner freedom.
—Deepak Chopra

January 23, 2003

I try to concentrate on the sun but find myself walking peacefully in a light fog. Then I see a tornado-shaped spiral descending into the earth. I know that I'm to go in, but I hesitate. My monk comes and gently encourages me.

I enter and find I'm not in the whirlwind I'd expected but gently floating. Inside is iridescent blue shimmering with colourful fireflies lighting all around me. I catch one with my right hand. Immediately, my hand and arm become warm. The same thing happens when other fireflies land on various parts of my body. I'm completely enveloped in such warmth and comfort as I float downward to the centre of the earth. The spiral narrows; I've come to the end of my journey.

I step out onto solid ground and walk along a path. I come to a set of French doors and enter a beautiful garden. There are white trellises with vines and flowers intricately intertwined. The trellises create an archway into a main walkway. There is a white wrought iron bench on the left and flower beds on either side of the path. A fountain at one end supplies all of the water needed for growth. The leaves, flowers and earth are their natural colours while the pathway and the fountain are light grey. Everything else is white.

I sit on the bench and know that this garden is key to my growth. It looks beautiful, but when I look closer, I can see all kinds of weeds. I have to pull them, but I'm not sure which are weeds and which are flowers.

I hear, "Start with the obvious."

I pick up a pail beside the bench and go to the first flower bed on the right side. I fill the pail with weeds and realize that I have just barely started weeding the whole garden.

"Do not despair. You can only weed so much each day, but you must tend to it every day."

I feel wonderful after weeding this small patch. I leave the garden and float up the spiral to the surface, where my monk meets me. I'm telling him my story when I see another spiral in the distance. This one is white and rising up from the ground.

I eagerly enter it and am greeted with an unbelievable sense of calm and goodwill as I float upwards ever so gently. When I reach the top, I climb onto a diving board and dive into the water. I'm swimming among the fish and playing with the dolphins. I see several seahorses. But then hundreds of seahorses of all different sizes surround me. The largest one catches my eye and indicates that I am to follow them.

We swim down to an underwater cave. When I look inside, the cave is full of gold coins, riches beyond belief. I'm disappointed; I don't want to be guided by materialism.

I hear, "This is spiritual, emotional, mental and physical abundance. Look deeper into the cave."

I see pathways and follow one to a barren room with one gold coin in the centre of the floor. I walk through this room into another stacked full of canned food. Through it, I find a third room that appears to be a meditation room. I carry on to a reading room with books lining the shelves. I keep walking and am full circle back to the chamber of gold.

"Behind this abundance are the chambers of humility and giving, nourishment, meditation, and reading for higher knowledge. Without going behind the golden chamber, you cannot fully encompass it and see all the riches that are here."

I thank the seahorses, step on to shore and go back down the spiral.

Once on the ground, I am met by all of the guides of my past meditations. We stand in a circle and sway clockwise around a central fire, giving and receiving energy from each other.

Discussion

The garden symbolizes my inner life; the flowers represent the thoughts of my Soul while the weeds represent my negative ego thoughts and beliefs. The weeds do not destroy the flowers, only cover them up. As with my alcove, I do not need a weed-free garden to experience inner peace. But the more I weed, staying committed, patient and compassionate with myself, the greater my inner peace will be.

The four chambers leading from the cave are the expression of my garden in my outer life. The room with a single coin represents humility from awareness of my Soul and giving fully of myself to others, with no ego attachment to anything in my life. The room full of food symbolizes nourishment from the joy of giving and from the physical and emotional freedom from the weeds I have pulled. The meditation and reading rooms offer guidance and learning from others.

The cave filled with gold coins symbolizes the all-encompassing abundance in my life that results from tending my garden: peace, happiness, joy, healthy relationships, success, good health. Each time I weed my garden, I cycle through the four chambers and encompass more abundance that awaits me in the cave.

Spirit has shown me that my outer life is the reflection of my inner life. My journey to inner peace is the means for improving my life.

10

SHIMMERING DIAMONDS

Nothing can dim the light which shines from within.
—Maya Angelou

January 28, 2003

The French doors of my garden are locked. It's dark, and I fumble with my key, dropping it in a pile of leaves. After searching with no success, I stop and say, "Please show me where the key is."

Immediately, I am led to it and open the door. The central trellised area feels smaller than before. I circle around where it's darker but still light enough to see flower beds, many overgrown.

A large tree grows against the outside wall of my garden. The flower bed from its base to the path is totally covered with weeds.

I hear, "The flower bed represents a period in your life; the weeds reflect the guilt you carry from that time."

I want to start weeding at the tree but wonder how I am going to get there without stepping on the flower bed. I move aside some weeds and see stepping-stones that I can use. There is a large fungus on the tree, which is a perfect height and size for a chair.

There are no flowers underneath as I pull up the weeds. But after clearing a patch, a flower starts to appear, uncurling like a fiddlehead to become a pale yellow/white snapdragon. It opens its mouth, and inside is a diamond that shimmers in the sunlight. Awestruck, I take out the diamond, turn it around in my fingers and then put it back. I continue to weed, and snapdragons appear all around, each one with a diamond in its mouth. Among these snap-dragons is a very large diamond embedded in the ground.

I finish weeding the entire garden using the stepping-stone paths to avoid trampling on any flowers. I begin to dump the pails of weeds into a larger bucket. I'm about to throw the weeds out when I notice that the bucket is becoming very hot and red.

I hear, "The weeds will just grow again unless you burn them and say farewell."

I step back to the main path to admire my new garden. All of the snapdragons open, and each of their diamonds cast a white glowing aura in the sunlight. I return to the base of the tree, its branches laden with bright red berries, and sit on my fungus chair. As I look out across my garden, I see the central trellis area brightly lit up and the gardens I have previously weeded looking radiant.

Discussion

Weeds of guilt associated with a particular time period of my life are so overpowering that this flower bed in the far reaches of my garden first appears dead, barren of any hope or beauty. But it is not. When I uproot enough weeds, I create space, an opening for a flower to reappear.

I marvel as a snapdragon unfurls and reveals its diamond within. The diamond represents my Light, my Soul. I metaphorically witness myself growing to remember my Soul. I hold the diamond but then replace it; I have not internalized that it is mine to keep—it is my Soul. As I continue to weed, the flower bed becomes resplendent with shimmering diamonds of my Soul, all surrounding the large diamond symbolizing Spirit.

No matter how guilty I try to make myself feel, I can never dim the Light within me. The flowers of my Soul are planted, waiting for me to have the courage to weed my garden.

11

ENTERING THE CAVE

Knowing yourself is the beginning of all wisdom.
—Aristotle

February 28, 2003

I settle into a cave. A bear comes lumbering in, eyes me and then walks over. I am not afraid, but it's very clear that I'm in his spot. I get up and move to the other side of the cave. I realize that his space is perfect for him, and my space is perfect for me. He tries to settle but gets up, walks to the opening of the cave, sniffs and looks around before re-entering. I follow suit.

The sky is a brilliant blue, the white snow is sparkling, and two birds are singing.

"Look further," I hear.

The trees are stripped of their leaves.

"Just as the trees are exposed to the elements and the world, you need to expose yourself, take off your mask and be your Soul. Mother Earth will protect you, and as with the trees, you will be reborn with new leaves."

I go back into the cave and notice that the bear faces all four directions before he settles. I face the South and see the Milky Way.

"All are One with the Universe."

I face the West and see a light.

"This is the source of Light with Its radiant beams."

I turn to the North and feel a tremendous downward pull of my eyes and head, so that I'm looking inside of my body.

"You need to look inward."

I feel unbalanced.

"You will only be balanced if you get rid of guilt and forgive yourself."

Finally, I face the East and see a white crescent-shaped light growing in size with each deep breath. I then see someone walking out of this light. I look further and see that I am the person.

Discussion

I am to enter the cave to shed my mask. I need to discover what my mask is made of and how to remove it so that I can blossom with new growth.

Facing the four directions leads me to be guided by my Soul, not my ego. The first two directions remind me that I am a Soul in the Universe, connected to Oneness. The third direction shows me that guilt is blocking me from experiencing this connection. My mask of guilt is a finely woven handiwork made by my ego. The fourth direction teaches me how to take off my mask. I need to breathe deeply to connect with my Soul, such as in meditation. With each breath, the connection with my Soul becomes stronger; my Light grows and replaces the darkness. I walk forward in life not from the darkness of guilt but from the Light of my Soul.

Healing is a journey of entering the cave to quiet my mind and body. I have been hibernating as the bear does in the winter—in a deep sleep, vaguely aware of my Soul but not fully conscious to It. When I awaken to remembering my Soul, I understand the wisdom I hold.

12

RADIATING

You are confined only by the walls you build yourself.
—Andrew Murphy

March 19, 2003

I see the double helix of my DNA.

I hear, "Take it out."

I hold my warm DNA strand in front of me. It radiates Light all around but not evenly. On the far side, the Light radiates evenly into the blackness until Its beam begins to fade further away from my DNA. But on the side nearest me, the Light stops abruptly, close to my DNA.

I walk around to the far side where my Light is radiating.

"This is the world unknown to you. You are impacting the world as you are intended, and the world is reacting to you as it is intended. On the other side is your known world—your life and how you see the world around you. You need to explore what is blocking your Light from radiating."

I walk back to the other side and venture out into the Light. I come to a set of black curtains. I open them and see a wall of large glass windows. With the curtains open, the Light now radiates through the windows.

"This wall is emotional fear," I hear.

The wall folds like a storefront, so I slide it into its enclosure.

I keep walking and come to a solid black wall, a pocket door in two sections.

"This is the judgement wall. The left side is others' judgement of you and the right side is your judgement of others."

I pry the wall open a crack and begin to push back the left side. It requires all of my energy and ingenuity. I need to find a stick to keep the wall open while I rest. I finally get the wall locked into place. I open the right side, my judgement of others. It is much easier to move, even a little easier than the wall of windows of emotional fear.

My Light radiates further, and I continue to walk. But again, I come to a wall, a thin curtain blocking the Light.

"This is lack of trust."

I easily open the curtain and see lines of bubbles rising in a large glass enclosure full of water, like an aquarium.

"This is love."

I step inside it and feel such love. I look out and see my Light radiating into the world as It is intended to do.

Discussion

My known world is life directed by my ego, where walls it has created block my Light. My unknown world is life guided by my Soul, unknown because I have not yet brought my meditations into my life.

Each time I open a wall, my Light radiates further until I am faced with another wall. I need to keep going, committed to my task of remembering my Soul.

With all my walls opened up, I am no longer confined or defined by them. I arrive at love, represented as air bubbles rising in water. Air in the bubbles supports my human life while I am embraced and surrounded by the water of Grace. My Light now radiates as It is intended to do.

13

CLUTTERED CLOSET

The essence of being human is
that one does not seek perfection.
—George Orwell

April 2, 2003

I ask any guide listening, "Why am I so focused on the negative things I've done and said? It seems as though I've opened the closet, pulled out a big box from the bottom and everything on top comes crashing down on top of me. I'm enveloped with all of my past negativity."

A guide appears and says, "There is more than the closet. Turn around and see the room."

I am in a pale yellow, circular room with full-length windows looking out to a cherry tree and crab apple tree in full bloom. There are no pictures hanging and not much furniture except for an area rug, an armchair, floor lamp and end table. Everything is in some shade of pale yellow.

There are two ways out of the room. One is a sliding glass door into the garden and the other, a front door with three steps down to a neighbourhood of houses surrounding a central lake. Each house is the same as mine, circular with a small closet extension.

"This is your bodily house, but you have only been looking into the closet. You need to get out of it, take one box at a time into your room and digest it, deal with it and throw it out. You have at least opened the door of your closet, but you must not stay there. It is everyone's goal over their lifetime to empty their closet."

I go back into my closet and take out the box dealing with some of my guilt for which I have already tried to make amends. But when I come back into the room, I see my younger self hanging, shackled, to the wall; I have still not released my guilt.

"You will not be able to move on from this until you let yourself down," he says.

I want to let myself down, but I feel that I would be doing it for my guide, and once he was gone, I would put myself back on the wall.

I say, "Maybe guilt isn't why I'm not letting myself down but rather my inability to accept human frailties, either in myself or in others."

My guide takes me outside and shows me two coffins. One is a rich mahogany and the other, a knotty pine. Yet, while the pine is "flawed," I don't see it as less appealing or beautiful.

He says, "These are only coffins housing the body. They will disintegrate over time. It is the Essence of the person that is key."

I am back in my circular room. It's packed with the auras of a large number of people. I'm also my aura, and as I move around the room, I notice some auras are white, some have breaks in their outline and others are multicoloured. I remove those with breaks and multicolours and bask in the harmony of being here with the seven remaining.

My guide comes in and asks me about this.

"I've eliminated the 'flawed' auras."

"You have given up on humanity. Humans are by their nature not perfect, never will be. They aren't supposed to be. It is your journey in life to learn from your mistakes and the mistakes of others and grow from both of them. By weeding out these other auras, you are not living your human walk. You need to accept being human and the necessary mistakes and lessons that this entails in both yourself and others."

I bring all the auras back into the room, and they intermingle. Then they take their physical form: a number I recognize but many I do not. One of the seven is Nicky, our most incredible dog.

"You know Nicky's unconditional love. He is your teacher. Enjoy, accept and honour being human."

I go over to myself hanging on the wall and undo the chains. My younger self slumps to the ground. I pick her up and we hug each other.

Discussion

This is the third time I have been in my quarters/house with a room and an alcove/closet. Here, the room of my Soul is calm and clutter-free. But the closet of my humanity is cluttered with boxes of guilt. I am living in the closet, unaware of the room behind me, with my ego in control. I need to remove my boxes from the closet and examine them from within the room, with the perception of my Soul, so that I can forgive myself.

In my life, I have concretely addressed a particular guilt—I brought this box into the room. Yet, I have only shackled myself to the wall. Underlying this guilt is my inability to accept human frailty in myself or others.

The rich mahogany coffin symbolizes life without human frailty; the knotty pine represents life as it is, human frailty etched in its wood. I see both coffins as equally beautiful because I understand that mistakes and weaknesses are part of living and that they do not impact our Soul within.

And yet, I do not bring this teaching into the room; I want only the purest, the rich mahoganies. We all have a house that surrounds the water of Grace—and we all have a closet in various states of clutter. We are all knotty pines.

As long as I am in human form, boxes will appear in my closet. I need to be attentive to the clutter. It is not that I am to overlook mistakes and weaknesses. Rather, I need to embrace them as learning opportunities in my journey through my life, not as a perfect human but as a human being.

14

WOLF TEACHER

The world as we have created it is a process of our think-
ing. It cannot be changed without changing our thinking.
—Albert Einstein

April 22, 2003

The waves are gently lapping the shore. There
is a tribal ceremony taking place with everyone in full costume. It is a healing circle for
me. I'm at the fire in the centre of the circle
and feel very peaceful.

Two of the healers lead me around the
circle where I have eye contact with everyone
except one man whose head is down. I stay
until he finally looks up. He has burning blue
eyes, and his headpiece is a wolf head.

We continue around the circle until I have
met all the healers before returning to the fire.

Seven from the circle join us and place their hands on me.

I return to the man with the wolf head. He opens his bag and drops out paper, a pencil and an eraser.

My wolf teacher says, "This is a magic pencil. You can't see what you write, but when you erase it, words appear."

I write, "I always have to be the best," but it doesn't show. I erase the area and see, "There is someone who will always do it better; just do the best you can."

I try a second time.

"I always have to have people know my success." Again, I erase it and read, "Success is on the outside; peace is on the inside."

He says, "Focus on inside of you. That is where you will find peace."

Discussion

For the first time in a meditation, a guide gives me a gift. Here, wolf teacher presents me with paper, a magic pencil and an eraser.

My self-critical thinking is invisible because it is not true to my Soul; it is created by my ego based on the past. The magic pencil teaches me what is true. But to access the lesson, I need to use the eraser—I need to be willing to change my thinking.

I need to remember to use wolf teacher's gift whenever my thoughts take me from inner peace.

15

LIFE MAZE

Attachment constrains our vision so that we are
not able to see things from a wider perspective.
—Dalai Lama

May 1, 2003

I ask for guidance on what I am to do with
my life.

Spirit comes in a bright Light. "You are to
enter a maze and find your way."

I enter onto a dirt path lined with holly
hedges. The sky is bright blue with a few fluffy
clouds. I notice that the path is half in shadow
and half in light.

Spirit says, "Everyone has a shadow side,
and you must acknowledge, embrace and
understand it."

I come to a three-way fork and ask my Inner Knowing which way I am to go. I enter an Inca trail with a stone path and moss-covered walls.

I come upon another crossroads and again ask the way I am to go. I enter a path of inter-locking bricks with tall cedars on either side. I look up and see a night sky with brilliant stars but still enough light to see. But then I become fearful of the dark.

"Just keep going," Spirit says.

Each step and movement feel like I'm in slow motion. Eventually, I see an azure sky with purples and pinks cascading and intertwining.

I come to another intersection, ask, and am directed to a path where I notice mice and squirrels scurrying around and spiders spin-ning their webs.

Spirit says, "This is your everyday life with activities and people you need to work with and be with, all the while still walking your path."

I eventually see the centre of the maze, like the hub of a large wheel with nine pathways entering from all angles. In the middle, there is a long stone bench with no sides or back.

I've entered at one corner of the bench. I wonder where is the best or right place to sit. With my back to the bench, I dance around it until I feel where I am to sit down, the far side of the bench. As I sit down, a guide approaches from the pathway immediately to my right.

"You wondered where the 'right' place to sit was. There is no right or wrong place. You do not always have to be right—perfectionism is harmful to you. What do you see in your line of vision directly in front of you?"

"I see two paths, and you standing on my right."

"Move down the bench and describe what you see there."

"I see different paths, and you're now to my left."

"Exactly. Your perception of truth is from where you are sitting. Move along the bench to get new perspectives that build on your previous ones."

I again ask what I am to do.

"You are to give more of your time, expertise and guidance. You have been given so much in your life. You need to give more than you have given."

Discussion

To discover what I am to do with my life, I need to make my way through my life maze with nine possible routes to the centre. It begins with the path of my healthy sense of self (the light side of the path) and my unhealthy sense of ego self (the shadow). From here, every combination of paths I take guided by my Inner Knowing results in different challenges and teachings. But I will always be given everything I need to safely make my way through.

I arrive at the centre of the maze but am still attached to doing the right thing; I see only the perspective in front of me and think this is the truth. I need to widen my perspective by including all views around the bench. When I do, I see as my Soul does—no path is better than another; they are simply different routes to the same end.

16

1 TIMOTHY 4

My course is set for an uncharted sea.
—Dante Alighieri

May 7, 2003

I am in my sacred forest of tall deciduous trees.

A guide walks toward me. He points to a large box not far off the path behind me.

He says, "You have discovered the gift, but you have only undone the beautiful bow and wrapping paper. You have not opened the box."

I am uncertain. I wonder whether I am ready to open the box, whether I can handle what is inside. I walk away but keep looking back at it. I finally decide I will open it and so turn back.

As I approach the box, it gets smaller and smaller until it's the size of a ring-sized jewellery box. I open the lid, and inside is a shining liquid Light, the Essence of Spirit, in a small perfume-shaped bottle. It sparkles and shimmers as I hold it up to the sunlight. I start to dab some on my arms and body but then realize that I am to drink it. As I swallow the liquid Light, I feel the energy, heat, Presence surge through my body. I know that I am radiant and glowing.

I walk along the road with this glowing Light inside me. People turn and smile at me, birds sing their beautiful songs and animals respond to me. All know I am filled with Spirit.

But then I think that this is just egotistical: "Look everyone, I'm chosen and filled with Spirit." I can't let my ego get in the way.

So I ask, "What am I supposed to do with this gift?"

My guide says, "You are to help people."

As I walk along, I see someone in the dark section of the woods beside the road. They are looking down and don't see me. I go to them; they still have their head down when I kneel in front of them. I lift them to their feet, guide them to the pathway and into the Light. They then look at me and smile and return to the dark woods to get their child and bring them out to the Light.

My guide asks, "Do you want to open your second gift?"

This time, I do not hesitate. I walk off the path into the woods and very carefully undo the beautiful bow, take off the shimmering gold foil wrapping paper and open the box. Inside is a Bible and underneath, a stack of sacred texts of all faiths.

I pick up the Bible and hear, "1 Timothy 4." I hear the words so clearly that I know this is something special. I thank Spirit for the gift as I put the Bible back in the box.

I return to the path and continue walking with my guide.

Discussion

By drinking the Essence of Spirit, I remember my Soul. I see the change in me, as does everyone and everything. I am to help others by guiding them from the darkness to the Light so that they remember their Soul and, in turn, help others to the Light.

However, what happens to me later differentiates this meditation from all others. I clearly heard "1 Timothy 4" in the meditation. But when finished, I wonder if there is even a book of Timothy in the Bible. I find a Bible and open it. Thunderstruck, I see 1 Timothy 4 right before my eyes. A shiver runs through me; I gasp, and tears swell in my eyes, as I know this is something special.

As I read Paul's letter to Timothy, I feel as though Paul is writing to me about how to be a good church leader;

I am to be diligent in the scriptures and speak openly of them so that I am an example for others and my progress evident to all. But I am uncomfortable with this because I do not want to be a church leader. My issue with 1 Timothy 4 stems from taking the scripture literally.

As I began to write this book, I have come to understand how the figurative message of 1 Timothy 4 is the culmination of the meditation lesson. Spirit is teaching me to follow the path I am on, stay diligent to my meditation practice and speak openly about what I have been taught. My journey will show others the process I have been guided through to live with inner peace.

"Life Maze" provided my life purpose, but I did not internalize it. Hearing "1 Timothy 4" in the meditation and opening the Bible to that exact scripture is Spirit's way of having me stand at attention—and I do. I have been very private about my meditations, speaking about them with only two friends. Now I understand that I need to be more open about my spiritual journey. The key going forward is how I act on this revelation.

PART TWO

Meditation is not to escape from society,
but to come back to ourselves and see what is going
on. Once there is seeing, there must be acting.
—*Thich Nhat Hanh*

17

CALL TO SUPPER

Don't let what you cannot do interfere
with what you can do.
—*John Wooden*

May 24, 2003

I am in a room with a long table covered by a white tablecloth, similar to pictures of the Last Supper. One of my ancestors welcomes me from behind the table. I'm surprised to see a relative who I hadn't thought had died sitting beside my ancestor. My relative is very happy.

Then more ancestors gather on the other side of the table; I sit by myself across from them. We have a lamb dinner and talk constantly. Everyone is having a good time.

When dinner is over and the others have left, I say to my ancestor, "I'm really glad that my relative is happy, but it's too bad I hadn't contacted them in life because I had been thinking about doing so for some time."

"The person is not dead yet."

"Good, I should call them then."

My ancestor hands me a black rotary telephone.

Discussion

A few years previous, there was a disagreement in my family. A relative on the other side of the disagreement is sitting with my ancestors. Metaphorically, without the connection we once had, my relative has passed on.

We are at a "Last Supper," a symbolic representation of the last time we would meet in person. This is the opportunity to do and say what needs to be done to heal wounds before spoken communication is no longer possible.

For the first time in a meditation, I am guided to take action—and I do. Right after my meditation, I phone my relative. I had told myself that I would not be able to call them, but Spirit tells me otherwise. By following my ancestor's guidance, I make the call and feel uplifted afterwards.

This phone call begins ongoing communication between my relative and me, each time more comfortable and meaningful.

18
GIFT EXCHANGE

For it is in giving that we receive.
—Francis of Assisi

May 28, 2003

I am dancing in a theatre where, every time I turn in a certain direction, I see a man in a dark suit with slick, black hair. He looks like a gangster. He comes up to me after the performance and wants me to join his dance troupe. I'm hesitant at first but then feel that he's a good man.

I join the travelling dance group, and for our first performance, we are in physical form. But for our next performance, we are beams of Light swirling around each other, making colourful shapes and designs. The audience's applause is in the form of flashing lights as their Essences "explode."

I ask to go to another dimension and find myself bathed in a peaceful, calm white. I can hear all the other Souls and feel their Presence. But I think that I need to return to physical form to learn more lessons.

I arrive in a forest. The path is illuminated, but the left side of the forest is in some darkness. As I walk along, I notice a gift under a tree in the dark area. The music seems rather sinister, so I think I had better avoid that present for the moment. I continue walking but keep looking back at the gift until I finally decide to open it. By the time I get back, the music seems lighter.

The gift is beautifully wrapped, and I take my time opening it. Inside is a flashlight. I turn it on and enter the dark forest. I scan the area in front of me and see the reflection of eyes and gnarled trees. I know I will be fine, but I still keep expecting to find something scary or gruesome. I never do and eventually walk through the forest into the bright sunlight.

I hear, "Spirit gave you a light to show you the way through the darkness. There is always light on the other side."

"Thank you for this gift."

I see another present lying in a grassy section at the edge of the forest. It's a smaller box, and without any hesitation, I carefully open it. Inside is a large wooden, rusty-red button. I wonder at this but then put it in my hand and start walking along the road.

Almost immediately, three men approach on foot with their horses trailing behind them. The one in the middle is large with a big potbelly and dressed in fancy old-fashioned clothes. His vest is missing the button I have. I give him his lost button, and he's so pleased. As a token of his enormous appreciation, he gives me one of the horses. I thank him and walk away with the horse.

I'm not very comfortable with horses, but in short order, I'm on the horse running wild; the two of us have become one. I feel connected to the entire animal kingdom.

I am riding by a field. The farmer is ploughing by hand, so I give him my horse to ease his work. In return, he gives me three ears of Indian corn.

I continue along the road carrying my precious corn when a 1920s Ford drives up.

"Can I give you a ride?"

At first, I'm hesitant but then accept. He sees my corn and asks, "May I have one for my daughter? She would really love it." I give him one. He drops me off in a town, and I go to a hotel.

I say to the manager, "These two ears of corn are all I have for payment. How long will I be able to stay with this?"

"You can stay as long as you like. The town will be ecstatic. With each of these kernels, we can plant corn and end our food shortage. The town is now going to prosper."

After staying in the town for a while, I decide to move on. The townspeople hold a party for me and give me a gold necklace with a circular sun pendant.

I am wearing my new necklace as I make my way along the road. I come to a crossroads and am guided to go down an empty road. I soon hear angelic choirs, and when I stop to soak in the sounds, a small boy appears.

I ask, "Can you hear the music?"

"No."

I take off my necklace and put it around his neck.

He says, "Now I can hear the angel music."

He gives me his love with a hug. This is my greatest gift. Love fills my body until I think I will burst. I am in a pool of unconditional love.

Discussion

My experiences as my Essence feel wonderful; they are the ends I desire, but I need more lessons to find my way to this inner peace in my life.

During the meditation, I am presented with a number of gifts. All gifts are for me, even if they are not for me directly. When I meet the man who needs my button, the gift exchange begins. Each time, I give to others exactly what they need, and they give me exactly what I need for my journey; we experience exchanges of unconditional giving and receiving.

Gifts, whether tangible or not, seemingly significant or not, are exchanges of energy. Each gift is a form of unconditional love. Each one flows, feels good and benefits everyone. These gifts may come in an endless variety of forms—a word, an intuition, a hug, a smile, material items. But I am to carry them with me, waiting for whomever or whatever I am to pass them along to. In return, what I receive back, again in a multitude of forms, will carry me along my path of giving and receiving to evergreater moments of unconditional love.

19

MY PART

Only if we understand, will we care. Only if we care,
will we help. Only if we help shall all be saved.
—Jane Goodall

July 9, 2003

I am flying over plains and fields, and then I
hover in front of a waterfall. I wonder what it
would be like to be a water droplet.

Immediately, I'm a water droplet free
falling over the cliff. I'm losing my stomach. I
plummet deep into the water before rising to
the surface. I'm jostled by rocks, relax in back
eddies and float down calm sections.

I'm telling the water droplets around me,
"This is like life: the rapids are the lessons
where you're jostled, tossed, disrupted; the
calm water is for reflection of the lessons
you've been through."

I feel a tugging upwards.

The water droplet beside me says, "It must be your time to evaporate."

I am drawn up to the sky.

I hear, "Do you want to help out in a drought?"

I think that it must really hurt when you hit the ground. But I say, "Yes," knowing that I must be needed there.

So again, I'm free falling, but when I hit the earth, it doesn't hurt; the splash of water is only my sweat that flies off. I'm going down into the earth and arrive at the roots of plants. Other people are here with hard hats and miner's lights frantically digging tunnels.

One says, "We need water to fill the tunnels."

I get a fire hose, turn on the water and fill the tunnels. All the plants survive.

I then meet a guide. "Look deep inside yourself."

I peer into my chest, squinting to see even deeper. I see a large seed with green growth sprouting.

"Everyone has the seed inside them. But they must awaken and let it start to grow. Yours is beginning. You will be amazed how fast it grows."

Discussion

I teach all the water droplets near me about the ebb and flow of life—just as I have been telling more people around me about my meditations after "1 Timothy 4." But Spirit calls me to evaporate, be my Soul, and asks me to help out on Earth; it is time for me to speak outside of my small circle.

I think what is being asked of me will hurt, but importantly, I understand that whenever I am called, I am needed. And, as is always the case, nothing that is asked of me will hurt me.

I am to help out in a spiritual drought. Many others have also answered the call to help. My part is to turn on the hose, share my journey further afield, so that water of Grace finds its way to nourish others for their own paths to inner peace.

20
THE CEREMONY

*We take spiritual initiation when we become
conscious of the Divine within us, and thereby
contact the Divine without us.*
—Dion Fortune

September 17, 2003

I am at the monastery with my monk guide
sitting on the bench in the garden. We walk
into the main hall. It is open with a large pillar
in each corner and one in the middle. The
marble floor, ceiling and pillars are all white.

A choir is standing in a line, chanting. I
sit on the floor facing them. I am thoroughly
enjoying the sounds and decide to join them. I
find that I know the chants.

I look down the line of monks to my left. A
young male monk at the far end of the line looks
back at me. I walk down the line to him, and we

look into each other's eyes. We hold hands, and I feel a warm surge of power enter my body.

The monk on one side of us puts his hand over our hands. The monk on the other side does the same, and the strength of this powerful sensation is wonderful. Then the entire choir circles us and puts their hands on ours. The sensation is even greater.

My monk and I go back to the bench. A large ball of Light appears in front of us.

He says, "It is an Essence. Do you remember all the fireflies you saw when you were floating down the spiral toward your garden? They were Essences."

My heart grows. My guide and I then transform from being in human form to our Essence; we are Light Beings. My guide's Essence is larger than mine.

"Why are our Essences different sizes?"

"Everyone has the Light within them; many do not know it. As you know, understand and live by this, your Light grows."

As I walk along, I give to everyone and everything around me. My Essence grows as I receive back more than I have given. I grow so much that I wonder if I will explode. But then I see that as I grow and touch other Beings and plants, they grow and, in turn, touch others. Collectively, we grow so much that we encompass everything. All is Light.

I realize that this is the meaning of the Light—the Oneness of everyone and everything. I now actually feel It and understand It in my heart rather than just in my head. Tears come to my eyes.

I stay as my Essence as I walk back to the monastery. Light Beings are holding rakes; others are ploughing the soil. We greet each other with a nod and hello.

Then I am back in human form dressed in monk's clothing. A monk greets me and hands me a teardrop-shaped, amber pendant on a necklace. We embrace and I walk on. Another monk gives me a very small scythe that fits into my hand. The next one gives me a two-headed hammer, another gives me a wallet and the last monk gives me a pen. I put all my gifts, my treasures, in a brown box and leave it outside the basement door of the monastery.

I enter the dark hallway and climb the steps leading to a trap door and the main hall. There is a party going on. All of the monks are laughing and dancing; one is dancing on his big toe. Their laughter is infectious. We continue to laugh as we form a circle with our arms around each other. When we move inward to the centre, there is almost an explosion, and a large white balloon rises up, bursts and then floats down to cover us in a dome-shaped lid of white.

Discussion

The first part of this meditation maps my journey to date. I enter the monastery as an observer, and the chanting calls me, just as my first Reiki treatment called me to begin my journey. I become my Essence, as I have done previously, but here, I take the next important step. I am initiated into the full acceptance of my Light and understanding of Oneness.

In the ceremony, I expand my Essence to the full expression of Itself. I do this by giving of myself to others and receiving back more than I have given. I move through the fear that giving will harm me by seeing that giving is infinite. I now feel and understand the meaning of the Light—Oneness of everyone and everything. I am moved to tears by the enormity of my experience.

Afterwards, I first see others only as their Light. Then I am dressed as a monk. I receive five gifts I neither use nor understand but which will play an important role in my future meditations.

I join in the celebration for me. The monks dance, their laughter infectious, as we honour my new life dedicated to living with the full awareness of the Light, of following my Soul. We draw together in a circle; our energies explode into a balloon that bursts and covers us with a white dome, representing the Light I experienced as my Essence.

I have taken a spiritual initiation of conscious awareness of my Soul and Oneness. My journey from here is bringing this awareness into my daily life.

21
TWO SIDES OF FORGIVENESS

When we forgive someone, the knots are untied
and the past is released.
—Reshad Feild

September 24, 2003

A guide says, "Go back to your very earliest memories."

I enter a circular cave, a bear's den. It's dark, although I can see a light at one end.

"Read the stories on the walls and write your own."

Each time I do, the light expands.

I then find myself lying face down on the floor of the monastery with the monks around me, chanting.

Someone I have issues with comes to mind. I then realize that a guilt I harbour stems from my doing the same thing I blame them for. I see the person tied down with ropes below me. I start to cut the ropes; my breathing is laboured. I don't know how many ropes there are or how many I've cut, but I keep going. After I loosen all of the ropes and forgive the person, I experience an incredible release. As the person rises up, they then loosen my ropes, and I am forgiven.

I feel forgiveness—the joy, the lightness, the peace. My body is tingling. The feeling lasts for a while and then disappears.

Another person is tied down. I blame them for involving me in an issue that I now regret. I'm able to cut the ropes faster than before. Once again, the person rises up and unties my ropes. I feel the wonderful sensation of forgiving them and being forgiven.

Then I am to forgive someone I have found challenging and now feel guilty for not understanding and helping them. I start cutting the ropes and become a bit disheartened that it's taking so long. I wonder why I'm not forgiving. Eventually, I free their ropes, and they rise up and untie me. Forgiveness floods over me. It doesn't last long, but what a feeling to strive for and truly understand and live by.

I leave the monastery with my monk guide.

I say, "That was different from my other meditations."

"You are ready for specific lessons. You need to focus just on them in order to progress along your journey."

Discussion

I am to write new stories from my earliest memories—not the contents of the stories but my reactions to them—so that the past no longer affects my present. Forgiveness is the means for me to do this.

Three times, I blame another person in my life for my guilt. Importantly, Spirit has chosen a wide range of relationship issues and guilt in my life, from significant to very minor. Regardless of the degree of hurt or guilt, the impact is the same. Whether I tie another down with one rope or a thousand, I am a prisoner just as I have made them.

When I untie each person, I forgive them; when they rise up and cut my ropes, I am forgiven and feel the joy, lightness and peace of forgiveness.

In the previous meditation, I left the gifts from the monks in a box outside the monastery. Am I here retrieving some of them, giving them a practical application? Amber, fossilized resin, holds my life history, perhaps helping me remember the events for the new stories I am to write. The scythe may be what I used to cut the ropes. Did I use the two-headed hammer to forgive? When the hammer rebuilds one side, it rebounds and rebuilds the other.

Forgiveness is understanding that nothing others or I have done has affected my Soul. I forgive by seeing the Light in others, and they reflect my Light back to me. Forgiveness is an act of freedom.

22

CALL TO ACTION

Obstacles are those frightful things you see
when you take your eyes off your goal.
—Henry Ford

October 7, 16, 2003

I say to my guide, "In the middle of the night,
I woke up and heard that I am to take another
action regarding the family disagreement. But
this morning, I question whether I actually
received this guidance."

My guide says, "Yes, you did."

* * *

I am in the monastery with my guide.

I say, "I thought carrying out my task would
be straightforward, but I'm running into unexpected challenges."

My guide leads me into breakfast, which is a bowl of worms.

He says, "They are very good for you. Sometimes you have to do things that are difficult in order to do what you know is right."

I eat a worm, and it tastes good. My food turns into appetizing spaghetti.

"Fear and uncertainty made your food look unappealing."

We are then at the edge of a grassy meadow overlooking the blackness of a deep valley.

He says, "For you to grow, you have to jump over the edge into the unknown."

I hesitate.

"The meadow is where you are living now; you know what your life is like here."

My chest is tight and painful. So, I decide to jump and move back to take a running start. As I approach, I trip on a root and fall. My second and third attempts are also blocked.

"The obstacles are stopping you from jumping over the cliff."

So, I just walk over to the edge and jump. I feel I'm in nothingness at first until I realize that I'm in a tunnel sliding toward the Light. When I get there, I feel a lightness; the pain in my chest is gone.

I wander along and come upon a gnarled tree. I climb it and find a comfortable place to lie down in a fetal position on a branch.

My guide asks, "How are you feeling?"

"I feel peace but not joy."

"That is because you are by yourself and not connected."

I leave the tree and seek out other Souls. I join them and find such joy in the Oneness.

Discussion

I receive instructions for a second call to action regarding the family disagreement four months after the first call. Unlike the ease of calling my relative, I run into unexpected challenges.

Spirit addresses my fear of these challenges with two analogies. In the first, my task is to eat breakfast; it is very good for me and the right thing to do. But my challenges make eating it unappealing. By tasting a worm, my breakfast transforms into appetizing nourishment.

In the second, my task is to jump off the cliff into the unknown. When I step back into the meadow of my life as it stands, no matter how willing I am to jump off the cliff, I stumble with each attempt. Only by standing at the cliff's edge am I able to take the leap of trust off the cliff.

I slide down into the Light, and my pain disappears. I come to a tree and rest peacefully in its branches. But I am not joyful until I connect with other Souls.

Spirit has given me the courage to act on my second task regarding the family disagreement. Once completed,

I feel contentment but not the lightness and joy I had anticipated. I need to connect with the Souls of those in the disagreement.

23

CALL TO CONNECT

Seeing other people in a different light
often reveals how much we are all the same.
—*Mark Amend*

October 29, 2003

I meet a pale-skinned, tall, thin guide wearing a long white robe. He's balding with deep set eyes and a Roman nose. We are on a bench overlooking a cliff.

He asks, "Are you in a deep meditation?"

"Yes, except for my eyes. They are not quite ready to relax."

"Even though you want vision, you are still holding back, afraid and uncertain of what you might see. Don't be afraid; just let go."

I do; immediately, my eyes relax. I turn to look at him, and he's distorted.

I ask, "What's happening to you? What are you doing?"

"I'm not doing anything. You are just getting vision."

I look around, and while everything still has its shape, it begins to become distorted, like looking into a ripple on the water or at a TV screen that needs to have the horizontal adjusted.

He says, "Keep looking at your hand."

Eventually, the distortions—or what I realize are vibrations—increase, so that all I see is light in the shape of my fingers and hand. When I look around, everything is an individual energy.

"You are now seeing with vision."

"This is wonderful but how can you function in the physical plane and only see energy?"

"You have to learn to slow the vibrations down enough to get the physical shape but not so that you lose its aura. Sometimes those who have the beginning of vision stop themselves because of fear when they see distorted faces. You have to work past this."

I lose my focus, and my guide calls to me, "Are you ready to come back?"

I rejoin him and bring up the family disagreement.

"You need to jump off the cliff with this baggage and let it go. But before you can do that, you have to keep the Souls of those in the disagreement with you."

I get very small dolls representing each person. As I look at each doll, a white Light circles it. I pick a piece of Light from each one and hold them together between my thumb and index finger.

"Place their Light in your heart."

As It enters my chest, I feel significant pain. But once the Light is inside my heart, the pain stops, and my heart expands and fills my whole body.

"Now you are ready to jump off the cliff with the baggage you carry."

The emotional weight of the disagreement is neatly packed away in a doctor's bag. I leap off the cliff and float down, letting go of the bag as I go. The bag plummets into the chasm. I continue to gently float and land in a warm pool.

As I easily climb back up over the bank, I am dripping wet with a smile on my face. My guide is smiling back at me from the bench.

Discussion

Spirit has offered me a trilogy of lessons involving a family disagreement.

For my third task, I again need to jump off the cliff, this time with the emotional weight I carry associated with the disagreement. But to do that, I need to bring the Souls of the others with me, just as when I was in the gnarled tree, I needed to connect with other Souls. I see the Light in each person and bring their combined Light into my heart. Now, connected with them, my heart fills my body. I jump off the cliff, let go of the weight and float gently into the water of Grace.

Spirit has led me through a three-part model for finding inner peace. First, I followed guidance. Second, I trusted guidance when following it seemed difficult. Third, I saw others differently so I could let go of the past. It is over time that I see how meaningful and effective this trilogy of life lessons has been.

24

THE VALUABLES IN
MY CLOSET

Sometimes letting go is an act of far greater
power than defending or holding on.
—Eckhart Tolle

November 11, 2003

I say, "I know I must continue to deal with my guilt, both what I consider major and minor because there is no difference."

Spirit says, "Give your guilt to Me."

"Won't I still have a memory of the event?"

"You will still remember the event, but you won't have an emotional attachment to it."

I am in my ego's house. It's dark but a gold purse laden with precious gems glistens in the darkness. Full and very heavy, I know it holds all of my guilt. Other items stand out in the room, but this is by far the most magnificent. I wonder how I am going to give up something as beautiful and precious as this. But I know that it is my ego desperately trying to hold on and keep me trapped under its control.

I walk out of the house with the purse over my shoulder, its weight bearing down on me. I meet Spirit in physical form. I try to give over the purse but can't let it go. I keep trying, and eventually release my grip. My body immediately feels like it's levitating, first my upper body and then my feet. I am so light and free.

Spirit says, "There is more that you need to surrender to Me."

I go back into the house, and although brighter without the purse, it's still dim. I can clearly see a gem-covered jewellery box and bring it outside to Spirit.

I say, "I don't know what's inside."

"Use your intuition."

"It houses all of my accomplishments."

"By giving Me the box, you will not lose your accomplishments or memories of them. You will only lose your attachment to them."

But my ego does not want me to give the jewellery box over and starts to fight back with chest pain; my successes are key to my ego's self-image. I realize my chest pain is only my ego, so I hand the box over to Spirit. The pain instantly stops.

Once again, I look around the house to see if there is more I need to let go. I know there must be but not what or where it is. Then I see on a table with many nondescript boxes a very small, heart-shaped jewellery box. While not as ornate as my previous two items, it stands out on the table. I hold the box in the palm of my hand, and my neck starts pulling to the right. The pain gets worse, extending all around my neck.

Spirit asks, "What is in the box?"

"I don't know. I just need to give it to You. I can't think with all this pain."

I rush over and give it to Spirit; the pain starts to dissipate.

Once the pain is gone, Spirit tells me to use my intuition for what the box holds. I do; inside is a choker.

"The choker cuts off your ability to connect to, and speak from, your heart. Put it on."

I wear it, and the pain is worse than before. I'm worried; I don't know if I'll be able to get it off. With it on, I'm totally unable to speak my truth or even know what's in my heart.

After a while, I am finally able to take the choker off, gasping, and give it to Spirit. The pain disappears, and I feel love throughout my body. I realize that this was the smallest and least ornate, but by far the most painful of my ego's three treasures.

Discussion

My ego's house is my closet/alcove. When I go outside it, I am in my room of my Soul, where I am able to let go of my ego's prized possessions.

My most difficult, yet most powerful, act is to let go of my guilt. Only then am I able to see my treasure of accomplishments, which I easily let go because of its pain. Again, only by letting go of that treasure can I find my most painful ego possession. The choker cuts off the connection from my mind to my heart, my Soul; I cannot understand what my Soul is doing and saying to me.

I have known about my guilt and my attachment to my accomplishments but not my choker. By letting go of the layers of the prized ego possessions I am aware of, I find ego treasures that lay hidden and cause me the greatest pain. Clearing my closet is a process of discovery and healing.

25

REASSURANCE

Trust your instincts. Intuition doesn't lie.
—Oprah Winfrey

November 12, 2003

I meet a Presence in physical form, but I can't distinguish any details.

"Someone asked me how did I know that I was communicating with good and not evil spirits. I was completely taken aback and didn't have any answer other than I felt nothing but goodness during my meditations. But how do I know?"

The Presence says, "Put your hand in this."

I move toward the bowl of what looks like molten lava and hold out my arm. I wonder how I could not be burned; the intense heat is searing my skin. I think, what if this is not Spirit but the darkness? This is exactly what

I'm asking guidance for. I go back over to the Presence.

"How will I know if you are Spirit?"

"Use your Inner Knowing."

I receive that It is Spirit, so I go back to the lava, comfortable that I will be safe. I put my arm toward the bowl and face the heat once again. When my hand gets to the lava, I discover that it is actually a soft, warm and soothing jelly. My body feels very warm, heavy and tingling. I lie down and know this is the feeling of Spirit.

I practise leaving the Presence's comfort and going back to the physical world. I am hesitant at first, as I am so peaceful and wonder whether I will be able to get back.

I think of all the things I need to do today and then ask to go back.

I run to the lava and plunge my hand into the centre. Immediately, I am back with the Presence. I try this several times to make sure.

The Presence says, "I will always be here. You can come to Me any time."

Discussion

As I have continued to share my meditations, someone questioned how did I know I have been communicating with good spirits. Without realizing it, I gave them the answer of my Inner Knowing; I feel nothing but goodness. But I need reassurance that I have been communicating with Spirit.

A Presence tells me to put my hand in molten lava. If this message is from the darkness, I will be burned. If it is from Spirit, I will be safe. Spirit uses these extremes to show me that I do know. My Inner Knowing is able to distinguish Spirit from the darkness and is available to me at all times.

26

BEAUTY

Take notice of what light does—to everything.
—Tess Guinery

December 3, 2003

I hear, "You need to see with another perspective, with vision."

I am floating in space, first in our galaxy, then another. I feel connected to everything and see beauty in all the stars, big and small. I am here for some time before coming back down to Earth.

I am lying on my stomach in the grass, examining a blade of grass; I see the blade as part of me. I notice a droplet of water on it and feel my connection to it.

I am in a meadow with a farmhouse in the distance. I walk slowly to it. While the farmhouse is old and dilapidated, I see only its beauty. I go inside. The broken glass in the window is in the shape of a star; the cracks in the mirror are rays of light. The lifting linoleum, the old metal chairs with plastic seats, the thread-bare plaid woven couch, the worn rugs, the slanted staircase, the crooked pictures on the wall up the stairs, the ragged curtains are all beautiful.

I enter the bedroom—mine, I think—and see an old chest with a dome-shaped top like a treasure chest. I open it and find a long white dress; it's cotton with eyelets, fancy but not ornate. At the bottom of the chest is a bracelet with pearls all around it.

Outside, I see a cloud of smog in the distance. But even it looks beautiful, with sparkling light throughout.

"How can it be beautiful when humans are creating a problem?"

I hear, "Everything has its beauty."

Discussion

In "Call to Connect," I found seeing with vision disorienting until I saw the Light of my hand. Here, everything I look at is beautiful because I am seeing its Light.

Inside and outside the farmhouse are my inner and outer worlds, respectively.

The broken, worn out, cracked, crooked, ragged items are my unhealthy thoughts and beliefs based on the past. With vision, I see only their beauty, their Light. The past has not changed but I have healed from all that was negative. The treasure chest holds a white gown and bracelet of pearls, both in good condition. Perhaps this is the dress I was wearing in the room of my Soul on the galleon in the first meditation of this book. Pearls are formed from healed wounds. The bracelet's circle of pearls symbolizes the completion of my healing.

I am confused by seeing the smog as beautiful; would this not condone or ignore our negative impact on the planet? But here, the smog is personal, those aspects of my outer life that are unhealthy for me—difficult relationships, life circumstances, what I do and how I act in my world that is not in my best interests or the best interests of others. When I see with vision, my smog does not disappear, just as the items inside do not physically change, but it sparkles with Light. Healing has taken place.

When I was in the non-physical realm in "Dance of Our Lives," Spirit gave me a precious gift of experiencing the awareness that we are Beings having a human experience. Here, Spirit goes a step further and demonstrates this treasured gift in the physical realm. I see the unhealthy aspects of my life through the Light of my Soul—everything in my inner and outer life is beautiful.

27

EARTH STAR

Vision is the art of seeing what is invisible to others.
—Jonathan Swift

December 19, 2003

Energy is pulsating through my body with electrical currents going to all of the nerves. It's like every nerve and cell is energized and awake. My body seems to be holding the energy in, so I leave my body, and the energy spreads out around me.

I am back in my body looking down a very dark, narrow tunnel and see a light at the end. I then realize I'm looking through a telescope and seeing with vision.

I see rolling waves and a beautiful sunset. I scan the horizon and see a sand beach. People are having fun, dressed only in loincloths, and making something together, a sandcastle perhaps.

I wonder about crowded cities and immediately find myself in Beijing. There is hustle and bustle, but when I look at the individuals, each has a beam of Light rising from their crown and around their head. All around I see the brilliance of all of these beams of Light.

I look around the world, and everywhere beams of Light are rising upwards, so that Earth looks like a star. I float above Earth to see this beauty, and then all of the beams focus and converge into my heart. I am connected to every beam, and the peace, love, joy I feel is transmitted to them. We are One.

I find myself at the end of the telescope again and wonder how do I keep this vision in my everyday life.

I hear, "You will learn to always see through this telescope, and eventually not need it as a reminder."

Then it's very dark; I am at peace. Spirit leads me through the darkness into the Light. I look at Spirit, who appears as a white man, then a woman, then a Black, then an Indian, then an Asian and then an Essence.

I sit with people around the world and look at them with love, compassion and joy. I know I need to pass on love in every aspect of my daily living.

Discussion

As a telescope is used to see the stars, here, the telescope is a symbolic tool for seeing the Light in others—seeing with vision.

In Beijing, I see the people but also beams of Light radiating from their heads. Beyond the city to the whole planet, everyone's Light fills the sky transforming Earth into a star of Divine Energy. I float up, and every beam of Light converges in my heart. We are all One, giving and receiving love and joy.

When I return, Spirit appears as both male and female as well as multiple races; everyone holds the Light within them. I sit with people from around the world, seeing them with love, compassion and joy, just as I experienced when we were beams of Light.

28
A QUESTION AND ANSWER

Listen to advice and accept instruction,
that you may gain wisdom in the future.
—Proverbs 19:20

January 22, 23, 29, 2004

"Spirit, what would You have me do?"

I cannot hear Spirit's voice. I feel I am willing to do what Spirit asks of me yet hear nothing but the chatter of my mind. Even when I am still, I hear nothing. I keep trying for some time.

* * *

"I know that being upset with those who said the wrong thing is keeping me from peace. Spirit, what would You have me do?"

But I do not hear Spirit. I start to doubt that I would even know if I were hearing Spirit or my ego. I can feel tears starting at my inability to break from my ego and stop all the chatter from my mind. This continues for some time as I try to still my mind.

And then Spirit takes my hand and leads me through the clouds. I think I'm deep in a meditative state, but Spirit says I have to go further. I need to duck down through a door, and then I'm in the Light. Now there is no doubt in my mind that I am with Spirit.

Spirit says, "Every time you are upset by something someone said, immediately send the person love, and the wrong will be gone, both in you and them."

The feeling of love throughout my body is incredible—peace, joy, stillness, lightness, happiness, contentment.

"Why could I not hear You yesterday?"

"You had blocked My voice because you were afraid of the answer to what you were to do. What you are to do now is send love back to each and every upset without exception."

I feel as though I'm still associating with my body.

Spirit says, "Leave your body."

Before, the love, joy, peace I felt was within my body with a glow surrounding my outline. But now, I have expanded beyond my body's form and become formless, like a gas escaping from a jar. Everything that I had experienced before is magnified and multiplied in intensity as I intermix with every Essence around me. I feel light and totally in bliss.

"Can I feel other Souls?"

I see a homeless older man lying on the cement. I help him up to a sitting position and, through his alcoholic breath, look into his eyes and see the Light. He looks into mine and seems to transform. I help him stand up, and with my arms around him, we walk down the busy city street. I feel nothing but love for this man, and his odour smells sweet to me.

We soon come upon a teenage prostitute. Again, I hold her shoulders, look into her eyes and see her Light. She looks into my eyes, stands tall and walks along with us, all of our arms around the others' shoulders.

Our steps do not waver. People intent on getting to work on time move aside with a look of wonder and disgust at my two friends. Ahead of us is a group of five businessmen. The CEO in the centre stops when I catch his eye and see his Light. He turns to join our group. His partners yell to him to turn around, but he continues with us, and very soon we hear none of their cries or see any of the negative looks of passersby. We rejoice in each other.

* * *

"Spirit, what would You have me do?"

"You are afraid of the answer."

"Yes."

"I would not have you do what you are unable to do. You lack trust. Come back when you have it."

Spirit leaves. I pray that my trust increases. I take a while to quiet my mind.

Spirit returns and says, "You have great potential and need to use it."

"Oh no, please don't tell me that I have some great thing to do. My ego is too strong. I'm trying so hard to get rid of it."

I start to cry.

"You are to teach."

I am quiet for a while. Spirit says, "You are doubting."

"Yes, because thinking I have great potential seems so egotistical."

"Quite the opposite; your ego will die. What you learn, you will give. Everything you do will be giving and for the good of everyone."

Discussion

I ask Spirit what It wants me to do. These three meditations form a trilogy about accepting Spirit's answer.

In the opening meditation, my question is so general and open-ended that my fear blocks Spirit's voice; I am not willing to listen to the answer. In the second meditation, even when asking for guidance on a specific issue, I am still initially unwilling to listen. In the third meditation, I immediately hear Spirit; I am now willing to listen.

While in the first meditation I hear only the chatter of my mind, in the second meditation, I am eventually able to listen to Spirit's answer to my specific question. I am to give love to everyone who I feel upset me. I experience the love, joy and peace of my formless Soul. And then, just as I did in "1 Timothy 4," I bring three people who are in their own version of darkness to the Light by reflecting their Light back to them.

In the third meditation of the trilogy, I am taken through the two stages of acceptance of the answer. First, although I am willing to listen, I still fear the open-ended possibilities. Spirit gives me one of my most critical lessons—I will only be asked to do what I am able to do. Only when I trust in this am I able to listen to the answer. I am to teach. The next step addresses my fears that arise. Hearing I have great potential feeds into my fear of egotism. Spirit teaches me that my ego fear is not true; when I teach what I have learned, I will be giving for the good of everyone, including myself. With this awareness,

I am then able to accept the answer. In writing this book, I understand the truth of Spirit's words.

Whenever I now ask Spirit for guidance, this trilogy gives the process for accepting the answer.

29

VENTURING OUTSIDE

Life begins at the end of your comfort zone.
—Neale Donald Walsch

March 30, 2004

Spirit, in physical form, and I are sitting in armchairs beside a beautiful fire. The room has burgundy leather chairs, dark wood panelling and Persian rugs. We are alone, and I feel very peaceful.

Spirit asks, "What do you think of the room?"

"It's dark."

"I see it as incomplete. Why don't you go and open the curtains. Light will complete the room."

There are seven sets of large black curtains. As I open each one and more Light fills the room, I become increasingly more peaceful.

When all are open, I notice I don't have to squint and that everything is visible. Looking out, I can see that the Light is coming from Light Beings, people's Essences.

I say to Spirit, "While I feel peaceful, I'm still inside, separate from the Light, only seeing It."

I walk outside and feel connected to the Light Beings. I am happy but keep coming back into the room where Spirit is sitting.

"I'm a bit concerned about having all these Light Beings connected to me, as I like my time alone."

Spirit has me go to New York. I'm jostled as I walk the crowded streets but am not connected to people. Then I go outside the room to the Light Beings, and it's a totally different experience.

The fire is burning low. I ask, "Is it time for me to leave, or should I put more wood on?"

"It is your choice. The embers are always here for you to put wood on and create a fire."

I put another log on, and we sit together in total peace. I go outside many times, further afield each time. One time, I feel what seem like tentacles reaching from my body. I touch another Light Being with one and send energy. An explosion of Light comes back to me. I receive much more than I have given.

Discussion

Although I am peaceful sitting with Spirit, the room is incomplete with the Light blocked. When I venture outside, I am happy being connected to Light Beings. Similarly, in "Call to Action," I was peaceful lying in the gnarled tree but found joy when I connected with other Souls.

But I do not understand how this connection translates into my life, worrying that it will affect my time spent alone. I mistake physical connection with Soul connection. Spirit demonstrates the difference by sending me to New York among the crowd of people, where I feel no connection with others. By contrast, outside of the room is completely different; I feel connected to all the Light Beings, never jostled but moving freely among them. Connecting with other Souls does not negatively affect my time alone, but rather adds to it.

I keep coming back to the room with Spirit because it is comfortable, familiar; being alone with my guides has been the foundation for my lessons from the beginning of my journey. But I venture further afield each time I leave the room and eventually send my energy to another, receiving back more than I have given. The more I connect with other Souls individually, the more my life is enhanced.

In my life, I am most comfortable being private about my meditations but have been cautiously sharing with more people since "1 Timothy 4." I need to go beyond this comfort zone. A new chapter of my life will unfold as I share my meditations more broadly and connect with others on a Soul level.

30

MY TELESCOPE

I have three eyes. Two to look. One to see.
—Bellamore

April 16, 2004

I have some trouble focusing. I tell my ego to please go away, but it keeps coming until I have to be even firmer with it. Eventually, it leaves, and I feel very relaxed.

I hear, "Look around you."

I turn around 360° but see nothing, only darkness.

"Use your third eye."

I look around again and still don't see much else until I gaze up and see what looks like a hole in the ceiling. I float up to it and go through what appears to be a dome-shaped structure I was in.

It's so bright that I think I'll need to squint or wear sunglasses but realize I don't. I float in the bright light and begin to move my arms. As I do, streaks of iridescent indigo, green, blue paint the sky. I make all sorts of designs with my body, legs and arms. The colourful designs stay for a while before eventually disappearing.

As I come down to my body, I float slowly back through the colours until I am in the darkness.

I am very peaceful and still. I then go through a door into a garden; I can smell the fragrance of the flowers. Just beyond the garden is a cliff down into a large valley. I look around and see that this valley surrounds the garden. The clouds in the valley are moving quickly, like storm clouds in fast motion.

"These are the storm clouds of life; they are part of life but will pass."

I turn back to the garden and enjoy its splendour and beauty. A butterfly lands on my hand. It flutters there for a while before hopping up my arm. It stops on my right ear and moves inside it a little. Then the butterfly flies over my head and lands on my left ear. I smile as its fluttering wings tickle my ear. It takes flight again and stops on my nose before going to my third eye.

It attaches to something that it pulls out of me as it flies backwards out from my third eye.

I can feel and see something cylindrical connecting the two of us; I am like a unicorn.

"This is the telescope of your third eye."

Discussion

Spirit guides me to see with my third eye, the gateway to see beyond what my eyes can see to the vision of my Soul. I am now able see a hole in the dome-shaped structure I have been in, my life confined by my physical awareness.

A butterfly flutters to my sensory organs before landing on my third eye, located between my eyebrows. It shows me that my third eye is my telescope; I no longer need an external one, as I did in "Earth Star," to see the beam of Light of everyone on the planet.

Whenever I look at others with only my two eyes, the picture is incomplete. I need to remember to use my third eye to see them differently, with vision that sees what my Soul sees—their Light.

31

GUIDANCE FROM MY HEART

It matters only that you love.
—Rod McKuen

June 2, 4, 16, 2004

I ask for help to get direction from my heart.

My guide says, "Go there."

My heart is completely entwined with wire.

"I can't find the end to unravel it."

"Keep trying."

I try for some time, still unable to find the end. Eventually, I find it and free my heart from the wire that has prevented it from growing.

* * *

I am sitting in the warmth and comfort of my heart.

My guide says, "Your heart is not big enough to hold all of your organs. You have released your heart, but it still has room to grow."

I am in one of my heart's chambers stretching the walls and mending any rips or holes. I have to sew very carefully. I can feel my heart growing and spreading.

* * *

My body is reversed: my skin is on the inside and my organs exposed on the outside. Little children keep coming up and touching my heart. I'm concerned that my heart will get damaged, so I put a glass cover around it.

I hear, "You are telling others to look but don't touch. You are keeping your heart to yourself."

I take off the cover and say to the children, "Take little pieces of my heart."

They do, and my heart starts to grow. My heart continues to grow as I extend it to more people until it becomes disproportionately large and circles my upper body.

Discussion

Spirit gives me a trilogy of lessons for receiving guidance from my heart, home of my Soul.

First, I need to free myself of the wires of unhealthy thoughts and beliefs that completely bind my heart. Not only do they prevent my heart from growing, they make it impossible for me to go inside it.

Once free of the wires, I am now able to sit inside my heart, but it is still not large enough to hold all of my organs, all of me. I need to expand my heart, finding the rips of hurt and sewing them with the thread of forgiveness.

Finally, I am inside out; I have grown, now opening myself to both others and myself. But I still believe I need to protect my heart. The glass cover does not protect me; it prevents me from giving and receiving love. By removing this final barrier of fear, I am able to offer my heart, my love, to others. As others take pieces of my heart, I am not diminished, but rather my heart expands with the love I receive to completely encircle me. My heart has grown to its "Soul" size, now holding all of me. From here, I live guided by my heart, my Soul.

32

GRACEFUL UNISON

You are the universe in ecstatic motion.

—Rumi

September 11, 2004

I am in a swirling spiral that I can feel throughout my body. But I'm attached to the ground and can't move or float.

"Something" takes a DNA strand from the top of my head and begins to unwind me. As the strand rises upward, my head shape begins to disappear, becoming a long white ribbon of undulating DNA. As the ribbon goes higher, more of my body unwinds—my shoulders, my arms, my torso, my legs, until I'm like a rhythmic gymnast's ribbon swirling up into the heavens.

I wonder what's pulling me. I look up, and above me are hundreds of white ribbons undulating. The rhythm changes to a dolphin motion. I'm being pulled up and carried along by their movement, the same as drafting in cycling. Then other ribbons form around me, all of us being lifted and propelled by the others' energy. We're flying, twirling, moving like waves in the heavens.

Then we close in and all go through a hole. In doing so, we become one mass of Light energy. We spread out over the tunnel like an umbrella. The white Light fills the whole vision of my mind. I am in this sea of Light, One with everything and everyone. I feel the Oneness but still with my own consciousness.

Discussion

In the previous meditation, my body was inside out. Here, I go further; I am freed of the complexity of my human-ness by the energy of other Souls, all of us individual *Grace*ful ribbons moving in unison. In "My Telescope," I floated up through a hole and moved freely, painting the sky with my body. Here, I join all the ribbons as we move through a hole and unite into one mass of Light that spreads out like an umbrella. I see myself and everything around me as One, as Infinite.

By unwinding my body, Spirit visually shows me that my Soul is both individual and part of the Oneness.

33

THE NEST

What we call results are beginnings.
—Ralph Waldo Emerson

October 8, 2004

I am carrying an envelope with "Forgive" written on it that I am to deliver to someone. I notice that it says "Forgive" and not "Forgiveness."

I hear, "The 'ness' comes later and is important."

I don't know where I'm to take the letter.

I am standing on a London-style narrow street with brownstones on a dark, rainy evening. People are driving cars, riding bicycles, couples are walking. I turn off the main road and deliver the envelope to someone, somewhere.

I am then in a light blue 1960s car. Spirit, in human form, is driving. We are on a dirt road with low lying fields on either side. The wind whips around us with the car windows open. No one is around; it's peaceful.

I say, "I haven't seen You in a while."

"I am always here. You just haven't come to seek Me."

I feel calm knowing that Spirit is always there.

We stop at a very steep mountain cliff.

Spirit asks, "Do you recognize this?"

"The valleys below are similar to those at the monasteries I've been at, but the mountain is much steeper."

I climb up the mountain alone; I need to use all fours. The top is a narrow apex with a magnificent view. I'm enjoying the view, but I'm drawn to four rocks in a semi-circle, each with one of the letters N-E-S-S.

I pick up the "E" rock. Underneath is an egg.

"It is new birth, new life."

I turn over the first "S" rock and find a sliver.

"A wooden stick was removed, and the pain is gone."

Underneath the "N" is a bird's nest.

"It houses and protects the egg. The sliver goes into the nest to help build it."

142

Finally, the last "S" rock reveals a star.

"The star guides you along your journey.

"To forgive brings you renewed life, freedom from pain, a new home to grow and protect you, and guidance along the way. They encompass the fulfillment of forgiveness."

Discussion

In "Two Sides of Forgiveness," I was taught that when I forgive, I release both the other and myself from the ropes that bind us. Here, Spirit adds to this teaching by distinguishing the "doing" of forgiving from the result—the "ness."

The nest, egg, sliver and star represent a new beginning, freedom from the past. I have everything I need for my journey to inner peace. I have a new home where I can safely grow to remember my Soul. Spirit's Light is always there to guide me to pull out each sliver of pain to build my nest stronger.

34

ON EAGLE'S WINGS

Bring into play the almighty power within you,
so that on the stage of life you can fulfill
your high destined role.
—*Paramahansa Yogananda*

October 19, 2004

I enter the front of a barn up at the level of the
rafters. They are close enough together to form
a bridge. I walk across the rafters to the back
corner of the barn where a woman holding a
baby sits cross-legged on a triangular platform
just big enough for them. As I approach, she
hands the baby to me, but I say, "No."

I walk back to the middle and sit on the
edge of a rafter. But it's frightening to be so
high up. I move back against the barn roof
to be more comfortable and notice that the
rafters are disappearing one by one. Soon they

will be gone, and although I can't see any solution, I think I will be saved. But I'm not and fall to the floor. The hay cushions my fall, but my ankle hurts. I look up and see the platform in the corner with the woman and baby.

I walk outside into the sunlight, assuming this is the Light I am to be in. But I keep looking back at the barn, sensing that I am to be up there and get the baby.

There is a huge ash tree at the front of the barn. I climb the tree and break the window in the peak. I cut myself getting in, but it doesn't hurt. But I'm on the opposite end of the barn from the woman and baby. There are no rafters, so I have to shimmy along the edge, my body pressed against the wall.

I eventually make it to them, and this time, I take the baby. The woman disappears, and I sit on the triangular platform with the baby. I have no idea how to get down or what I'm going to do. I sit in silence for what seems like an unusually long time.

Eventually, a train comes along right through the barn roof. I board the train with the baby, sit down across from a man wearing a bowler hat and contemplate the English countryside scenery.

We arrive at a station, and I get off with the baby. Everything is totally white—people's faces, their clothing, the walls. I think that this is the Light. But I have no idea where to go. I just stand there with the baby until a woman comes along, takes my arm and leads me away. But we never get anywhere.

The baby and I are back on the train, going in the same direction. We get off at the next station, which is also white, but the platform is narrow and leads down a staircase. I start down but don't feel comfortable and so come back up and get on the train.

The next stop is back in the barn, and so I get off and again sit on my triangular platform with the baby. I sit and sit and sit and sit. The baby never ever makes a noise. At some point, I feel pressure on my forehead as if I'm wearing a bandana. Still nothing happens, and I can see no way down.

But then I see a ladder going along the roofline and rising up to the peak of the roof. I'm surprised that I hadn't seen it before. I take the bandana off and use it to tie the baby on my back. I climb up the ladder and open the trap door at the top of the roof. The 360° view is beautiful.

An eagle comes by, picks us up and flies across the land. The sensation of flight is intense and releasing, as I had become tense during this whole ordeal. We eventually land in the eagle's nest. Inside, there is writing paper, art paper, pencils and pens.

The eagle picks me up to go and get food. We fly to a river and dive down into the water. I'm sputtering and spewing as we come up. The eagle has a salmon.

When we fly back to the nest, the eagle tips the salmon and drains its blood into the writing materials.

I hear, "The salmon's blood is the food for writing and drawing."

Discussion

The barn represents my life meditating in the rafters but living on the ground floor, unable to fully connect the two. I have made progress in Part Two, but I need to get out of the barn altogether to incorporate my meditations into my life.

The first time I leave the barn, I walk alone out from the ground floor; I have not applied the lessons. My Inner Knowing tells me I need to go back to the barn and get the baby, my inner child. My journey going forward will include her.

The second time, I leave with the baby from the rafters. We board a train, and twice I think I have found the Light I seek. But each time, my Inner Knowing tells me I need to go back to the barn. Meditating, by itself, will not lead me to inner peace.

The third time, I finally feel the bandana and see the ladder, the tools Spirit has given me to get out of the barn;

I will always be given the exact tools I need. I climb with the baby through a trapdoor in the roof and now have the full perspective of my life. I am out of the barn but still attached to it.

The eagle comes and flies us to the nest of forgiveness I learned about in the previous meditation. From the safety and guidance within the nest, I will be able to incorporate my meditations into my life.

The nest is full of writing materials, including the magic pencil, eraser and paper from my wolf teacher and the pen from the monk. In "1 Timothy 4," I learned that I was to help others through sharing my journey. Here, I am given the expression of this sharing. My books are the realization of Spirit's plan for me.

The eagle flies me to get food from within the water of Grace and pours the blood of a salmon into the writing materials. The salmon's blood will nourish my Discussions, revealing the wisdom of Spirit's teachings and the interconnectedness of the meditations. The salmon knows to return home. In the same way, my deeper understanding of the meditations has brought me closer to returning home and remembering my Soul.

This meditation signals an expansion of my role. I have been, and will continue to be, taught by many guides in my meditations. Spirit is showing me that the time has now come for me to assume the role of a guide to help others find inner guidance for their journey. My meditations are not mine but they are for me, as they are for others. It was not my idea to write my books or to become a guide, but I acknowledge and accept my role with gratitude.

POSTSCRIPT

Most, if not all of us, have experienced those moments that take our breath away, that leave us marvelling at the mystery of life. I had such an experience just before publishing this book that I would like to share with you.

I went out for an early morning kayak paddle in a very dense fog. For my hour trip back to shore, I decided to paddle down the middle of the lake using a compass bearing that just popped into my head. About halfway back, the fog lifted around me, and soon a white rainbow appeared, its two ends dipping into the lake with just the hint of colour. I marvelled at this phenomenon I'd never seen or even heard of before. I paddled under the rainbow back into the fog and continued toward shore. Shortly before I arrived, the fog lifted, and to my sheer amazement, my compass bearing took me back to my precise launch spot, not a degree one way or the other. I knew that I'd been both guided home and shown that Spirit was with me as I finished this book.

I am humbled and eternally grateful for the guidance, in all forms, I have received. My difficult relationships have been healed, my guilt minimized and, although my journey is ongoing, I live with inner peace—at least, most of the time.

Thank you for reading *True Compass*. I hope you have found guidance within it for your own path to inner peace.

ACKNOWLEDGEMENTS

Dennis Denomy, as my editor, you encouraged me to look at my writing from the reader's experience so that, in your words, we would be as two pilgrims on a shared journey. You also taught me that fewer words create more powerful and meaningful Discussions. Your commitment to this book has been a blessing to me, and I am forever grateful to you.

Heather Murray, Jennifer Murray, Lynda Smith and Debi Tziatis, thank you for your time and thoughtful feedback on an early manuscript. Heather and Lynda, thank you also for proofreading my book.

Donna Taylor, I am grateful for your insights and dedication to detail on my final draft.

Joey Mauro, as my publishing specialist at FriesenPress, you have been attentive, helpful and encouraging throughout my publication progress. Thank you for holding my hand.

Everyone I've met throughout my life, from my most intimate relationships of family and friends to my more casual ones, has played a role in creating this book because we've all impacted each other's lives. I thank all of you, for without our connection, I never would have experienced the joy of the incredible journey I've been blessed with.

9 781525 596537